© Wyatt North Publishing, LLC 2013

Publishing by Wyatt North Publishing, LLC. A Boutique Publishing Company.

"Wyatt North" and "A Boutique Publishing Company" are trademarks of Wyatt North Publishing, LLC.

Copyright © Wyatt North Publishing, LLC. All rights reserved, including the right to reproduce this book or portions thereof in any form whatsoever. For more information please visit
http://www.WyattNorth.com.

Cover design by Wyatt North Publishing, LLC. Copyright © Wyatt North Publishing, LLC. All rights reserved.

Scripture texts in this work are taken from the *New American Bible, revised edition*© 2010, 1991, 1986, 1970 Confraternity of Christian Doctrine, Washington, D.C. and are used by permission of the copyright owner. All Rights Reserved. No part of the New American Bible may be reproduced in any form without permission in writing from the copyright owner.

About Wyatt North Publishing

Starting out with just one writer, Wyatt North Publishing has expanded to include writers from across the country. Our writers include college professors, religious theologians, and historians.

Wyatt North Publishing provides high quality, perfectly formatted, original books.

Send us an email and we will personally respond with 24 hours! As a boutique publishing company we put our readers first and never respond with canned or automated emails. Send us an email at hello@WyattNorth.com, and you can visit us at www.WyattNorth.com.

Foreword

Christian Writing Decoded provides the reader with a detailed history and analysis of the most important Christian writings.

Saint Augustine of Hippo has long been a central figure to Christian thought, informing both on the nature of God and the nature of Christian morality.

The treatise *On Grace and Free Will* is one part of a much larger conversation that Augustine was having with other priests and leaders within the North African church. The text is rich in history, and is an important read for Christians and historians.

This book provides an original history and analysis of *On Grace and Free Will* coupled with an appendix.

About Wyatt North Publishing...3

Foreword...4

On Grace and Free Will Decoded...9

    Introduction..10

    North African Geography and Church Polity.............................12

    The Appearance of Cœlestius in North Africa............................14

    Augustine Introduced to Pelagian Views......................................16

    Direct Correspondence Between Augustine and Pelagius......18

    Pelagius on Trial 19

    Trouble in Adrumetum..21

    Augustine's Method of Scriptural Interpretation.......................23

    The Argument of the Work as a Whole..25

    The Occasion for the Work and the Letters to Which it was Attached (Chapter 1)...26

    The Relationship of God's Commandments to Free Will (Chapters 2-5)...28

    Chastity and Free Will (Chapters 7-8)..30

    Prayer and Free Will (Chapter 9)...32

    Grace and Merit (Chapters 10-17) 34

    Eternal Life and Grace (Chapters 18-21).....................................36

    The Law and Grace (Chapters 22-27)...37

    Faith and Grace and Free Will (Chapters 28-30).......................39

    God's Commandments and the Fulfillment Thereof (Chapters 31-33)..40

On Grace and Free Will 49

    Chapter 1 — The Occasion and Argument of This Work. 50

Chapter 2 — He Proves the Existence of Free Will in Man from the Precepts Addressed to Him by God. 50

Chapter 3.— Sinners are Convicted When Attempting to Excuse Themselves by Blaming God, Because They Have Free Will. 51

Chapter 4.— The Divine Commands Which are Most Suited to the Will Itself Illustrate Its Freedom. 52

Chapter 5.— He Shows that Ignorance Affords No Such Excuse as Shall Free the Offender from Punishment; But that to Sin with Knowledge is a Graver Thing Than to Sin in Ignorance. 53

Chapter 6 — God's Grace to Be Maintained Against the Pelagians; The Pelagian Heresy Not an Old One. 55

Chapter 7.— Grace is Necessary Along with Free Will to Lead a Good Life. 56

Chapter 8.— Conjugal Chastity is Itself the Gift of God. 56

Chapter 9.— Entering into Temptation. Prayer is a Proof of Grace..58

Chapter 10 — Free Will and God's Grace are Simultaneously Commended. 58

Chapter 11.— Other Passages of Scripture Which the Pelagians Abuse. 59

Chapter 12.— He Proves Out of St. Paul that Grace is Not Given According to Men's Merits. 60

Chapter 13 — The Grace of God is Not Given According to Merit, But Itself Makes All Good Desert. 61

Chapter 14.— Paul First Received Grace that He Might Win the Crown. 62

Chapter 15.— The Pelagians Profess that the Only Grace Which is Not Given According to Our Merits is that of the Forgiveness of Sins. 62

Chapter 16 — Paul Fought, But God Gave the Victory: He Ran, But God Showed Mercy. 63

Chapter 17.— The Faith that He Kept Was the Free Gift of God.....64

Chapter 18.— Faith Without Good Works is Not Sufficient for Salvation. 65

Chapter 19 — How is Eternal Life Both a Reward for Service and a Free Gift of Grace? 65

Chapter 20.— The Question Answered. Justification is Grace Simply and Entirely, Eternal Life is Reward and Grace. 66

Chapter 21 — Eternal Life is Grace for Grace. 67

Chapter 22 — Who is the Transgressor of the Law? The Oldness of Its Letter. The Newness of Its Spirit. 68

Chapter 23 — The Pelagians Maintain that the Law is the Grace of God Which Helps Us Not to Sin. 69

Chapter 24 — Who May Be Said to Wish to Establish Their Own Righteousness. God's Righteousness, So Called, Which Man Has from God. 70

Chapter 25 — As The Law is Not, So Neither is Our Nature Itself that Grace by Which We are Christians. 71

Chapter 26.— The Pelagians Contend that the Grace, Which is Neither the Law Nor Nature, Avails Only to the Remission of Past Sins, But Not to the Avoidance of Future Ones. 72

Chapter 27 — Grace Effects the Fulfilment of the Law, the Deliverance of Nature, and the Suppression of Sin's Dominion. 73

Chapter 28.— Faith is the Gift of God. 73

Chapter 29.— God is Able to Convert Opposing Wills, and to Take Away from the Heart Its Hardness. 74

Chapter 30.— The Grace by Which the Stony Heart is Removed is Not Preceded by Good Deserts, But by Evil Ones. 75

Chapter 31 — Free Will Has Its Function in the Heart's Conversion; But Grace Too Has Its. 76

Chapter 32 — In What Sense It is Rightly Said That, If We Like, We May Keep God's Commandments. 77

Chapter 33 — A Good Will May Be Small and Weak; An Ample Will, Great Love. Operating and Co-operating Grace. 79

Chapter 34.— The Apostle's Eulogy of Love. Correction to Be Administered with Love. 80

Chapter 35.— Commendations of Love. 81

Chapter 37 — The Love Which Fulfils the Commandments is Not of Ourselves, But of God. 82

Chapter 38.— We Would Not Love God Unless He First Loved Us. The Apostles Chose Christ Because They Were Chosen; They Were Not Chosen Because They Chose Christ. 83

Chapter 39.— The Spirit of Fear a Great Gift of God. 84

Chapter 40 — The Ignorance of the Pelagians in Maintaining that the Knowledge of the Law Comes from God, But that Love Comes from Ourselves. 85

Chapter 41— The Wills of Men are So Much in the Power of God, that He Can Turn Them Whithersoever It Pleases Him. 86

Chapter 42 — God Does Whatsoever He Wills in the Hearts of Even Wicked Men. 88

Chapter 43.— God Operates on Men's Hearts to Incline Their Wills Whithersoever He Pleases. 90

Chapter 44 — Gratuitous Grace Exemplified in Infants. 91

Chapter 45 — The Reason Why One Person is Assisted by Grace, and Another is Not Helped, Must Be Referred to the Secret Judgments of God. 92

Chapter 46 — Understanding and Wisdom Must Be Sought from God. 93

On Grace and Free Will Decoded

Introduction

The treatise <u>On Grace and Free Will</u> is one part of a much larger conversation that Augustine was having with other priests and leaders within the North African church. Although very rewarding reading on its own, it can be like hearing only one half of a telephone conversation.

Augustine's thoughts and concerns that he raises in this treatise are best understood in the wider context of the theological disputes in which the church was engaged at the beginning of the fifth century. The church had already taken a stand regarding the pivotal textual, theological, and Christological controversies that emerged very early in church history. In A.D. 325, the council of Nicæa had rejected the Arian view and affirmed the full divinity of Christ (First Council of Nicæa). In A.D. 367, Athanasius had circulated his 39th Festal Letter that solidified the church's New Testament canon with the twenty-seven books that we today identify as the New Testament (Letter 39).

For the last fifteen years his life or so, Augustine was embroiled in a theological controversy with other monks in North Africa. Having resolved the church's position on the nature of God and the nature of Christ, this new controversy revolved around the nature of man. It is called the Pelagian controversy after Pelagius, the original proponent of the heretical view. The New Testament writings contain an inherent dichotomy between the human capacity to exercise free will in the decision to follow Christ and not to sin and the divine grace involved in that decision. Early theologians recognized the presence of both processes, but might chose to emphasize one aspect over the other as the need arose.

The problem Augustine identified in the teaching of Pelagius was not simply that he emphasized free will at the expense of divine grace, but rather that by emphasizing free will in such a dramatic way Pelagius negated the Fall and the human need for divine grace in the first place. In speaking of the controversy, the Presbyterian theologian B. B. Warfield put it this way,

10

> The real question at issue was whether there was any need for Christianity at all; whether by his own power man might not attain eternal felicity; whether the function of Christianity was to save, or only to render an eternity of happiness more easily attainable by man.

Several synods were held throughout the Holy Roman Empire that declared the views purported to belong to the Pelagians as heretical, whether the Pelagian leaders on trial in these synods were condemned as heretics or not. Eventually, after being cleared by multiple tribunals, Pelagius himself was branded a heretic.

But the seeds had been sown and from time to time these views would reemerge throughout Christendom. Augustine wrote the treatise <u>On Grace and Free Will</u> in response to theological questions along these same lines that emerged in a secluded monastery in North Africa. He was 72-years old when he wrote this treatise and had already designated his successor, whom he had asked to help in relieving some of his responsibilities. (Letter 213)

North African Geography and Church Polity

In the historical proceedings that surrounded the Pelagian controversy several actors in the controversy hold ecclesiastical titles with defined roles within the church of the fifth century. The office of the "deacon" belonged to those who helped distribute the Eucharist and dispense the alms collected by the church.

Those with the privilege of consecrating the Sacrament of the Eucharist held the office of "presbyter." The office that today goes by the name of "parish priest" was filled in the fifth century by deacons or presbyters who were appointed to serve in one particular rural church and the duties of this office grew over the centuries.

Just as it is today, it was the "bishop" who presided over the deacons and presbyters as well as the laity within a large geographic region demarcated as a diocese. Local monasteries in the fifth century were also under the purview of the bishop, who appointed the abbot who oversaw the day-to-day operations of the monastery. "Metropolitans" were bishops of important cities with apostolic origins who exercised authority over the bishops of the Provinces. These metropolitans were responsible for convening Provincial Councils and presiding over the same.

Augustine spent most of his life in North Africa and a little orientation to the geography of the region during the fifth century will help in following the events that surrounded his treatise <u>On Grace and Free Will</u>. Augustine was born in a highland region in what is today Northeast Algeria, in the city of Thagaste. One of Augustine's close friends, Alypius, became the bishop of Thagaste in A.D. 394. One year later, Augustine became the Bishop of Hippo. Hippo is the ancient name for a province in the northeastern corner of Algeria about 60 miles west of the Tunisian border on the Mediterranean Sea. Hippo Regius was the name of the main city within the wider region of Hippo that lies 60 miles north of Thagaste.

As a prominent seaport, Hippo Regius was a prominent trading center for Roman ships along with Carthage. Carthage is the ancient name for Tunis, the capital of Tunisia, which lies at the northern tip of Africa along the Mediterranean Sea. The churches in the city of Carthage were under the care of Bishop Aurelius during the fifth century. Carthage belonged to the larger region of Uzalis. Evodius was the bishop of this region during that time. One hundred miles south of Carthage lay the city of Adrumetum (also spelled Hadrumetum), modern Sousse, also on the Mediterranean because the continental edge cuts north-south at that point. A large monastic community lived in this city under the care of the abbot, Valentinus.

The Appearance of Cœlestius in North Africa

Augustine may never have entered the Pelagian controversy had it not been for political instability in Rome. The British born Pelagius was around the same age as Augustine and had been teaching his heretical views quietly in Rome for many years in relative obscurity along with his younger friend Cœlestius.

In A.D. 410, Paulinus, the bishop of Nola, wrote a letter to Augustine asking for clarification on some difficult verses that were being used by these two. It would take Augustine four years to reply to that letter. Meanwhile, that same year, Alaric I, King of the Visigoths, having already destroyed much of the Roman Empire, sacked Rome itself and besieged it for the third and final time. This historical event forms the climax of Edward Gibbon's famous work, The Decline and Fall of the Roman Empire. With Rome in ruins, Pelagius and Cœlestius fled to Africa in A.D. 411. Pelagius himself did not stay long in Africa and travelled instead to Palestine, leaving his friend Cœlestius behind in Carthage.

Cœlestius wanted to continue his ministry in Carthage and asked to be ordained as a presbyter there. This request made its way before Paulinus of Milan (not to be confused with the aforementioned Paulinus of Nola), who was living in Carthage while he was writing the biography of Ambrose, the bishop of Milan, whom he had served as deacon for many years. Paulinus recognized his name as one who had been reported to be teaching heresies while in Rome and in an attempt to put a stop to the spread of heresy into Africa, he accused Cœlestius of seven points of theological heresy.

Aurelius, the bishop of Carthage, convened a synod where he and Paulinus asked Cœlestius to answer the church regarding his position on these seven points of doctrine. Augustine transcribed segments of the proceedings of this synod in his treatise On Original Sin. In this proceeding Cœlestius did not deny the accusations that Paulinus made against him, but only questioned their basis. For this reason, Aurelius and this Carthaginian synod excommunicated Cœlestius denying his request to be appointed a presbyter.

Not to be detoured in his efforts to continue his livelihood in service of the Church, Cœlestius then sailed to Ephesus where they granted his same request and ordained him a presbyter.

Augustine Introduced to Pelagian Views

During the brief period that Pelagius was in North Africa, he visited Hippo, but at a time when Augustine was absent. Augustine also notes that they saw each other in passing while Pelagius was in North Africa, but the two never had a conversation. At the time, Augustine had heard rumors that Pelagius "had disputed against the grace of God." (Proceeding of Pelagius, 46) When Augustine returned to Hippo and inquired about Pelagius, those who had spoken with him had not heard him say anything that would confirm the rumors.

Augustine was very careful and measured in his response to heresy and he did not want to condemn the viewpoints of others without hearing or reading firsthand their own positions. To this point he still had not responded to the letter from Paulinus of Nola asking about certain difficult scriptural passages cited by the Pelagians. Moreover, Augustine had his hands full addressing the Donatist controversy that was affecting Africa directly, whereas Pelagius had gone to Palestine and was no longer a local concern in the region.

While arguing against the Donatists at a conference of Catholics and Donatists held at Carthage in A.D. 411, Augustine had become close with Marcellinus, who presided over those proceedings. This friendship was advantageous for both men, since Marcellinus was acting in the capacity of the secretary of state of the Western Roman Empire. One year later, Marcellinus wrote Augustine with questions about the various Pelagian views. The questions can be listed as follows:

1) Would Adam have died if he had not sinned?

2) Is Adam's original sin passed on hereditarily?

3) Are infants baptized for the forgiveness of sin?

4) Have there ever been or will there ever be a person without sin at all?

As was his custom, Augustine replied to these questions with a 2-book treatise, which consists of the first two books of <u>On Merit and the Forgiveness of Sins, and the Baptism of Infants</u>. After he had completed this treatise, Augustine obtained a copy of Pelagius' commentary on the Pauline epistles that contained other arguments that Augustine had not addressed. He subsequently wrote an appendix to this work, which consisted of a book in its own right—book three of the aforementioned treatise.

Ever the eager student, Marcellinus wrote Augustine with a follow-up question regarding a point made in the second book of <u>On Merit and the Forgiveness of Sins, and the Baptism of Infants</u>. Marcellinus was confused about Augustine's assertion that a sinless life was indeed possible, while still maintaining that no person had ever or would ever be able to live such a sinless life. This question produced yet another treatise, entitled <u>On the Spirit and the Letter</u>.

Direct Correspondence Between Augustine and Pelagius

It is important to note that Augustine continually strove to correct Pelagius rather than discipline him. He had a passion for orthodox doctrine within the Church and believed that with compelling arguments he could persuade others to his views. He spoke of Pelagius respectfully, "a holy man, as I am told, who has made no small progress in the Christian life…" (Merits and Remission of Sin, and Infant Baptism, iii 1).

The following year, A.D. 413, Augustine received a letter from Pelagius directly. The content of this letter is unclear other than that it contained several praises of Augustine and his righteous life. Augustine replied with an uncharacteristically short letter (146) downplaying Pelagius' praise of him asking instead that Pelagius would pray that Augustine would indeed become the man described in such glowing terms by Pelagius and asking for God's grace to be bestowed upon Pelagius by means of good deeds and eternal life. This two-fold view of the consequences of divine grace is a theme Augustine explores at more length in On Grace and Free Will (Chs. 20-21).

Much to Augustine's chagrin, Pelagius turned around and produced Augustine's letter at the Synod of Diospolis in his own defense. Augustine later asked, "Wherefore, then, did he produce this letter at the trial?" (On the Proceedings of Pelagius, 53)

Having now written multiple treatises against the Pelagian heresy and having corresponded with Pelagius himself, Augustine was finally able to write a long letter (149) in reply to Paulinas of Nolan's questions concerning the difficult to understand statements of Paul in his epistle to the Romans.

Pelagius on Trial

In A.D. 415, Augustine sent a letter to Jerome who was living in Jerusalem by the hands of Paulus Orosius. When Orosius arrived, John of Jerusalem was presiding over a synod and asked Orosius both about Pelagius who was now living in Palestine and serving the church. John also asked about Cœlestius, who had been condemned at the synod in Carthage and was known to be a student of Pelagius. Orosius recounted the proceedings of the synod at Carthage concerning Cœlestius as well as the treatises Augustine had written to Marcellinus refuting Pelagius' positions that appeared in his writings. John of Jerusalem called for Pelagius asking him to explain his position regarding the possibility of humans leading sinless lives in this world. John of Jerusalem was not comfortable ruling on this matter and referred the case directly to Rome. (Orosius, Apology for the Freedom of the Will)

Shortly thereafter, two deposed bishops living in exile in Palestine brought a formal accusation against Pelagius. This formal accusation reached the metropolitan, Eulogius of Caesarea, who convened a synod of 14 bishops to review the matter at Diospolis. On the date of the synod, the two bishops who brought the charge were ill and unable to attend. The accusation written in Latin remained, but since the region was Greek-speaking, none of the bishops in attendance could read the accusation, so a translator rendered each heading of the accusation into Greek as they arrived at it.

Pelagius read several letters addressed to him by prominent members throughout the Holy Roman Empire, including the letter from Augustine. Since Pelagius seems to be the only one at the synod aside from the translator who was fluent in both Greek and Latin, the synod could find nothing for which to condemn him and cleared him of the accusations of heresy. (On the Proceedings of Pelagius)

With this result, Pelagius was overjoyed and shortly thereafter published In Defense of Free Will. As soon as news of this synod reached North Africa, the bishops there held two provincial synods where more than sixty bishops at each condemned the teachings of

Pelagius and Cœlestius highlighting the tension between West and East and the church politics that ensued cannot be taken lightly.

Five of the North African bishops including Augustine sent a letter to Pope Innocent I asking him to examine carefully Pelagius' teachings, along with letters from their two recent synods that had condemned Pelagius and Cœlestius. Six weeks before his death, Pope Innocent I (a Roman pope with a western orientation) replied to these letters favorably that he agreed with the African synods and condemned Pelagius' view on infant baptism and excommunicated Pelagius and Cœlestius.

Practically as soon as Pope Zosimus was installed in his office, Cœlestius came in person asking that Zosimus overturn his predecessor's decision to excommunicate him. He then received letters from Pelagius and Praylus, the bishop of Jerusalem, writing on Pelagius' behalf. Pope Zosimus, a Greek by birth, and thus eastern in orientation, wrote two letters declaring Pelagius and Cœlestius orthodox, thus overturning the prior decision by Pope Innocent I.

This action provoked the ire of the North African bishops who assembled in Carthage 200 strong to ask Pope Zosimus that the excommunication of Pelagius and Cœlestius remain until they be willing affirm the following statement, "we are aided by the grace of God, through Christ, not only to know, but to do what is right, in each single act, so that without grace we are unable to have, think, speak, or do anything pertaining to piety."

This power play by the North African bishops made Pope Zosimus nervous and he agreed that the decision of Pope Innocent I would stand for the time being. Not only did the North African bishops brandish the stick; there is evidence that they supplied a carrot as well. One of the Pelagian heretics that Augustine corresponded with later, Julian of Eclanum, accused Augustine's friend Alypius of bribing Pope Zosimus, while on a mission to Rome at this time, with eighty Numidian stallions (Unfinished Work I, 42). A few short months later Pope Zosimus issued an imperial decree banishing Pelagius and Cœlestius from Rome.

Trouble in Adrumetum

By A.D. 422, the Pelagian controversy seems to have quieted down in the Church. Pelagius had been condemned as a heretic and the views of the Church had been solidified regarding these theological questions. To differentiate matters, historians refer to the controversy that follows as the 'semi-Pelagian controversy.'

Two letters from Augustine (214 and 215) that were sere sent along with the treatise <u>On Grace and Free Will</u> and the reply he received to these letters (216) explain the circumstances that produced this additional controversy. In A.D. 426, two monks named Florus and Felix departed from their monastery in Adrumetum on a journey of charity to Uzalis, where Florus had been raised. One of their stops during this journey was to the library of Evodius, the bishop of Uzalis. In Evodius' library, Florus came across the letter from Augustine to Sixtus (Letter 194) that discusses prevenient grace. Florus was so edified by this letter that he obtained a copy for himself and sent it with Felix back to their monastery in Adrumetum to edify their brethren, while he continued his journey to Carthage. When he arrived, Felix read aloud Augustine's letter to his illiterate brethren, which greatly offended at least five of the monks who thought that Augustine, in his zeal to protect divine grace, left no room for free will.

When Florus returned from his journey of charity, his brethren attacked him for stirring up such division within their monastery. In trying to defend himself, Florus appealed to the abbot, Valentinus, who had not been present during the reading of Augustine's letter and had been unaware of the resulting dissention among his monks. In an effort to resolve the conflict, Valentinus sought the advice of three local Church authorities: Evodius, the bishop of Uzalis; Sabinus, a priest who is otherwise unknown; and Januarius, a priest from a neighboring town. Valentinus presented the replies of all three of these local authorities to his monks, which appeared to them to lack any theological substance and did nothing to change their positions on the question.

Believing he had taken every other step possible to end this conflict, Valentinus sent two of his monks, Cresconius and Felix, on a journey to Hippo Regius to ask Augustine himself to clarify his letter to Sixtus that had created such controversy in their monastery. Although there is no direct testimony to this effect, these two monks may have each represented opposing sides of the controversy.

The two monks appeared before Augustine without any introduction or commendation from Valentinus, but carrying with them only Augustine's letter to Sixtus, which had created the controversy and which they hoped to have explained (Letter 215, 3). Augustine was very gracious with them, listening to their story and explaining in much detail both his letter to Sixtus and the Pelagian controversy in which the church had been embattled for several years that formed a backdrop to that letter. The monks were anxious to get back home to their monastery before Easter armed with a letter from Augustine for Valentinus and the rest of their brethren (Letter 214), but just as they were about to leave, a third monk from their monastery, also named Felix, joined them delaying their departure. This subsequent delay allowed Augustine more time to explain the Pelagian controversy and to copy many of the documents surrounding that controversy for reference by their monastery. Ever vigilant, Augustine composed an additional longer letter to Valentinus (215) along with his treatise <u>On Grace and Free Will</u>.

Augustine's Method of Scriptural Interpretation

For Augustine, the basis for any theological argument is the Holy Scriptures. He emphasizes their role in his treatise in his introductory letter to Valentinus (214) in the following way, "Therefore I have in this letter, which has reached you, shown by passages of Holy Scripture, which you can examine for yourselves…" (Par. 4) In examining the treatise On Grace and Free Will it is important to note how Augustine takes various scriptures from both the Old and New Testament and applies them to the question of the relationship between human free will and God's grace.

One of Augustine's favorite tools in interpreting scripture is to propose an alternative way to phrase a sentence. He uses this exegetical tool multiple times throughout this treatise. The apostle Paul could have said "X" but instead he said "Y".

The alternative statement that he proposes is one that fits the interpretation Augustine is in the process of refuting. He then proceeds to contrast this alternative statement with the actual scriptural statement. The alternative statement may leave out a few words as in "Watch that you enter not into temptation" versus "Watch *and pray*, that you enter not into temptation" (Ch. 9); or it may substitute a few words as in "I have obtained mercy *because I was* faithful" versus "I have obtained mercy *in order to be* faithful" (Ch. 28). This type of interpretation is to be expected with his extensive training in rhetoric. Before turning to the Church, Augustine held a position as "imperial professor of rhetoric" in Milan (O'Donnell, James J. "Augustine: His Time and Lives," in The Cambridge Companion to Augustine. ed. Eleonore Stump and Norman Kretzmann [Cambridge: Cambridge University Press, 2006] p. 17).

In other instances Augustine's focus is on the underlying implication of a particular statement. He may focus on the meaning implied by the use of particular vocabulary or he may focus on the implications behind certain syntactic constructions. In chapter 4 there is a good example of this latter, where Augustine collects a large number of commands scattered throughout the whole of scripture to make his point—namely that the social implication (or expectation) behind any command is that the recipient is capable of obeying that command.

Another common method of interpretation he uses is that of key-word association. One word that appears in one context may also appear somewhere else in scripture in a different context. By looking at both passages together, Augustine illuminates one passage with the aid of another. In one example, he provides a different interpretation of Romans 3:18 than that supplied by the Pelagians. Typically, the term *fidem* "faith" is understood as a characteristic of believers within the Church. Augustine pairs this verse with James 2:19 where the verb *credunt* "believe" is applied to the demons making a semantic connection between the two terms, Augustine demonstrates that Paul's statement in Romans 3:18 can be aligned with Paul's other statements in the epistles to the Romans and Galatians by interpreting this instance of the term "faith" in light of James' use of the term "believe."

The Argument of the Work as a Whole

Augustine wrote this treatise very much like a commentary on his letter to Sixtus (Letter 194). Augustine intended these two texts to be read side by side or at least with the earlier letter in mind. In this treatise Augustine is not addressing Pelagians, but rather faithful monks who are confused about the relationship between grace and free will—thus the term 'semi-Pelagian controversy.' Augustine's approach in addressing their concerns is to highlight biblical passages that affirm the reality of both grace and free will in the life of the Christian.

The major tenets of Augustine's position in this treatise are that every person has free will, which was created by God with Adam. Once Adam sinned, human free will became distorted or tainted by this original sin. This sinful nature causes people when given two options to choose the sinful option. But God offers his help and grace to allow people to choose righteousness and obedience. God then rewards this choice of righteousness with eternal life.

The Occasion for the Work and the Letters to Which it was Attached (Chapter 1)

The first chapter to <u>On Grace and Free Will</u> combined with the two letters to Valentinus (214, 215) is what allows for a reconstruction of the historical situation that occasioned this work. The historical reconstruction is presented above and need not be repeated here. The goal of this section is rather to focus on the literary aspects of these letters and the introductory chapter that were not relevant for the historical reconstruction.

In his first letter to Valentinus (214), after reviewing his experience with the monks whom Valentinus had sent, Augustine first identifies the primary thesis of his treatise and the impetus behind it.

> I wish you to understand in accordance with this faith, so that you may neither deny God's grace, nor uphold free will in such wise as to separate the latter from the grace of God, as if without this we could by any means either think or do anything according to God,—which is quite beyond our power. (Par. 2)

Here Augustine explains to Valentinus his concern for the monks under the abbot's care. In respect to God's grace, he fears they will deny it; with respect to human free will, he fears they will promote it irrespective of grace. It is for this reason that most of his treatise is spent promoting and highlighting the role of God's grace and downplaying human free will. In his first introductory letter (214), it is only in closing that he reaffirms the presence and the importance of human free will.

In his second introductory letter, Augustine notes the many literary resources that he is sending to the abbot for the edification of his monastery concerning the Pelagian heresy and the Church's response to it. In addition to these resources, Augustine informs Valentinus that he read through St. Cyprian's work <u>On the Lord's Prayer</u> (Treatise 4) with Cresconius and the two Felix's and implies that he would have copied this work as well for them had they not informed him of its existence in their library. Here again, it is only after he has highlighted the importance of the grace of God that he exhorts Valentinus and his monks to upright living (Par. 5-8).

The Relationship of God's Commandments to Free Will (Chapters 2-5)

After the necessary introductions and preliminary matters, Augustine first and foremost affirms the existence and necessity of human free will. The first argument he makes is that the divine commandments would be useless without human free will.

He then seeks to prove this proposition with two separate points. Human free will, moreover, is what allows for the divine commandments by providing knowledge of sin to render people inexcusable with regard to their sin (Ch. 2). Despite the "inexcusable" position, people continue to excuse themselves for their sin (Ch. 3). The point being that if one were to deny "free will," the apostle Paul would not be able to declare that people are without excuse. In this way, Augustine further clarifies his own extended discussion of this topic in his letter to Sixtus (194, 22-29).

For his second point, Augustine cites a multitude of direct commands from both the Old and New Testament as proof of human free will (Ch. 4). God would not be able to command these things if there were no "free will."

Having affirmed the existence of free will, Augustine then explains his chief concern in his discussions with the Pelagians. Here he is commenting the following statement from his letter to Sixtus,

> When they think they are being deprived of their free will if they admit that man has no good will of his own without the help of God, they do not understand that they are not thus strengthening human free will but puffing it up… (Letter 194, 3)

To the Adrumetum monks he explains that his main fear is that in trying desperately to maintain free will that the Pelagians leave no room for the grace of God. This would allow a Christian to glory in himself because of his righteous life, rather than glorying in God, whose grace made that righteous life possible.

This conclusion is not just a theoretical concern on Augustine's part. He was, in fact, very careful to read their writings carefully before entering this controversy. Augustine quotes Pelagius' treatise <u>On the Grace of Christ and on Original Sin</u> as saying, "For his willing, therefore, and doing a good work, the praise belongs to man…" (Book 3). It was clearly this conclusion that Augustine was concerned the monks of Adrumetum might reach.

Chastity and Free Will (Chapters 7-8)

Continuing his discussion of the relationship between the commandments and free will, Augustine brings up the special case of chastity. He knows that chastity is one of the vows these monks have all taken and since by this point he has written so extensively on the subject of sexual desire in relation to the Pelagian controversy this provides him a means of sharing a glimpse of his views on that subject.

He begins by quoting Jesus' view on the subject from the Gospel of Matthew when he affirmed the disciples sarcastic retort that it would be better not to marry. He then moves on to cite the apostle Paul's exhortation in his first letter to Timothy that the young man remain chaste. Augustine highlights for the monks that this statement from Paul was directed to Timothy's free will by implication. But he argues that one need not only rely on implied statements from Paul, since in his first letter to the Corinthians Paul makes direct reference to the will-power exercised by a young man towards his fiancée. To this point, the monks at Adrumetum who have been emphasizing free will would likely be following along with Augustine's argument as supporting their own view.

But Augustine then makes an interesting exegetical move with these two passages, interpreting the one in light of the other. The reason there is no scriptural reference following the final quote in Chapter 7 is that Augustine is not actually quoting Jesus here, but 'misquoting' or 're-quoting' him. Using Paul's statement in Corinthians, Augustine takes the common noun *potestatem* 'power,' as in 'will-power,' from Paul and makes it the subject to the verbal phrase *datum est* 'is given' that was indefinite in Jesus' statement in Matthew. Jesus' phrase "to whom it is given" becomes "to whom the (will-)power is given." In this way, Augustine argues that the thing that is given is 'will-power,' which, according to Jesus is available to some and not to others.

In Chapter 8, he then elaborates on this point by arguing that God appeals to free will when he forbids both fornication and adultery, nevertheless, it is only by grace that men are able to keep these commandments. To support this point, Augustine quotes the Wisdom of Solomon with its affirmation that "no one could be continent, except God gives it" (8:21). As the conclusion to this discussion, Augustine lays out his bottom line point on the relationship of God's commandments to free will. God's commandments (including chastity) are directed towards the will power inherent within individuals. But this will power is weak and unable to keep these commandments without God's grace.

Prayer and Free Will (Chapter 9)

In his treatise entitled On the Proceedings of Pelagius, Augustine records the minutes from the Synod of Diospolis held in A.D. 415 where Pelagius was examined for his teachings. The Synod quoted a letter from Pelagius to widow where he instructed her to pray in the following manner,

> He worthily raises his hands to God, and with a good conscience does he pour out his prayer, who is able to say, "Thou, O Lord, know how holy, and harmless, and pure from all injury and iniquity and violence, are the hands which I stretch out to You; how righteous, and pure, and free from all deceit, are the lips with which I offer to You my supplication, that You would have mercy upon me." (On the Proceedings of Pelagius, Ch. 16)

It is likely this sentiment that prompted Augustine to make the following statement regarding prayer to Sixtus,

> Therefore, the very act of prayer should not take credit to itself, even if help is granted to him who prays to overcome his covetousness of temporal things and to love eternal goods and God Himself, the source of all goods, for it is faith that prays, faith which is given to him who does not pray, for, if it were not given he could not pray. (Letter 194, 10)

Here Augustine cites a statement where Jesus is chastising his disciples for their inability to stay awake during a time intended for prayer. The statement is then made "Watch and pray, that you enter not into temptation" (Matt. 26:41). Augustine then points out the possibility that Jesus could have made a legitimate complete statement using only one of these verbs. Using the first verb exclusively would have appealed to the disciples' will, whereas using the second verb alone would have appealed to God's grace in avoiding temptation. The use of both verbs underlines the importance of both divine grace and human will in avoiding temptation.

Grace and Merit (Chapters 10-17)

In paragraph 6 of his letter to Sixtus, Augustine says of the Pelagians, "even when…they admit to receiving some divine help…they claim some previous merit of their own…Thus they think their merits precede His action…" Augustine then goes on to cite multiple biblical passages supporting his antithetical view of the subject. Because Sixtus, to whom he was writing, was in agreement with Augustine on this position, there was no need for Augustine to elaborate on why the Pelagian position was flawed.

But when he addresses this same point with the Adrumetum monks, who are flirting with this position, he is much more careful in his argumentation. Here he either cites or anticipates the actual scriptural support the Pelagians use for their position. Immediately, he reiterates a point that he had made to Sixtus that Pelagius himself renounced this view (that the Adrumetum monks seem to be flirting with) as anathema. But not be seen as excusing Pelagius, Augustine adds further, just as he had with Sixtus, that the later writings of Pelagius demonstrated that this reply to the direct questioning of the Palestinian bishop was disingenuous. His mention of Pelagius again in this context, serves to underscore how gravely serious this theological issue is to the church. The concept of merited grace is heretical.

Returning to their scriptural citations, Augustine first considers the oracular statement made by the Lord of hosts in Zechariah, which has the form "Do X, and I will do Y." He does not dispute that this is a consequential statement with the second half both following and dependent upon the performance of the first half. Here he argues that this passage is simply a close-up snapshot of one series of events. Were one to zoom out the camera, as it were, and see what falls outside of the frame, an additional event or proposition would appear—namely that it is God who allows a person to "do X" in the first place. He supports this with several quotes from the Psalms and a further statement of Jesus.

Augustine then turns his attention to two passages from the book of Chronicles interpreted by the Pelagians in favor of merited grace. Here again he freely acknowledges that these two verses affirm human free will. He does not try to argue for a different interpretation of these verses, but rather puts them in the wider context of the entire scriptures. First he cites the apostle Paul's statement that reward for merit is simply the payment of a debt and not grace. He then proceeds to cite an example from Paul's life itself. Augustine reminds the monks at Adrumetum that the Apostle Paul mercilessly persecuted the Church of God before his conversion and therefore had an evil merit that warranted punishment not reward. But it was in this state and at this time while Paul merited only punishment that God extended his grace to the apostle, which converted him (Ch. 12).

One of the reasons that emphasizing free will had become so popular in ascetic communities was that these communities were continually seeking the sinless life. With this in mind, Augustine notes that the grace that God bestows on sinners that leads them to justification is not a one-time event. God continues to extend this grace on a daily basis to those who have already been justified (Ch. 13). Returning to the example of Paul's life, he cites Paul's affirmation toward the end of his life where he summarizes his merits in the Christian life to Timothy. For these merits, Paul states that he hopes for a heavenly crown. Augustine then comes full circle arguing that the only reason why Paul can boast of these merits is because of the grace he was afforded while his own merits were evil. The conclusion Augustine draws is that even these latter merits would not have been possible without the preceding divine grace.

Eternal Life and Grace (Chapters 18-21)

In his letter to Sixtus, Augustine anticipates an objection to his line of argumentation as follows,

> The objector says to this: "But men who refuse to live uprightly and faithfully will excuse themselves by saying: 'What wrong have we done by leading a bad life, since we did not receive grace to lead a good life?'" (Letter 194, 22)

In clarifying this previous letter to the monks at Adrumetum, he says "Unintelligent persons…have thought [Paul] to mean that faith suffices to a man, even if he lead a bad life, and has no good works." (Ch. 18) To this line of reasoning, Augustine compares this type of faith without good works to the faith of the demons spoken of by the Apostle James. True faith, Augustine argues, results in both good works and eternal life.

It is then only by understanding this two-fold consequence of divine grace that it is possible to understand Jesus' statement in the Gospel of Matthew that God rewards good works [with eternal life]. Since the good works themselves are a result of grace, even though the immediate cause of the gift of eternal life is good works, the ultimate cause of this gift is grace. Therefore, eternal life is not something earned or merited, but rather "grace for grace."

The Law and Grace (Chapters 22-27)

The impetus that seems to have given rise to Pelagius' heresy was the desire to live an upright and righteous life and to encourage his fellow Christians to do the same. Augustine in no way wants to dampen the ardor of those who desire to live righteously and in light of God's grace. He, therefore, exhorts the monks of Ardumetum to live uprightly in accordance with the law given in both the Old and New Testaments. This leads him to take up the extended discussion of the apostle Paul in his letter to the Romans focusing on the nature of "the law." Augustine first contrasts what Paul actually said, "the law is the knowledge of sin" with what Paul could have said, but didn't that "the law is the *destruction* of sin." After citing extensive passages from Paul's letters to the Romans and the Galatians, Augustine informs the monks of Adrumetum that the Pelagians argue, "the law is the grace of God" in opposition to this testimony by the apostle Paul.

In this case, we have roundabout confirmation of this teaching from Pelagius himself. Pelagius wrote a book entitled <u>Defense of the Freedom of the Will</u>. Copies of the book itself have not survived, but a portion of that book can be reconstructed from the extensive quotes contained in Augustine's two-book work <u>On the Grace of Christ, and on Original Sin</u>. In chapter 8 of book 1, Augustine provides the following quote from Pelagius, "And this grace we for our part do not, as you suppose, allow to consist merely in the law, but also in the help of God." In defending his own position, Pelagius protests that he does not consider grace to only consist of the law, but also to include the help of God. In so defending this position, Pelagius affirms his belief that "the law is the grace of God" as Augustine has phrased it in this treatise.

Augustine is flabbergasted that they could be reading the same scripture as he and yet come to the conclusion that the law can be equated with grace. Part of the confusion on this point between the two may result from their focusing on two different parts of scripture. It is clear that Augustine is focusing on the Pauline epistles to refute Pelagius on this point. The starting point that led Pelagius to this conclusion was likely not the Pauline epistles, but the book of Hebrews with its list of Old Testament saints. This is evident from one statement in a letter from the Pelagians sent to Rome clarifying their position. Augustine provides this quote in his work <u>Against Two Letters of the Pelagians</u>, "We say that the saints of the Old Testament, their righteousness being perfected here, passed into eternal life,—that is that by the love of virtue they departed from all sins…" (Ch. 39).

Another quote from Pelagius himself was the "The kingdom of heaven was promised even in the Old Testament." (<u>On the Proceedings of Pelagius</u>, 13) This latter quote Pelagius affirmed in the Synod of Diospolis and supported citing scriptural proof from the book of Daniel. The synod indicated their assent that this viewpoint was indeed the position of the Church.

Here again Augustine adjures the monks of Ardumetum to live uprightly according to their free will. He then asks that when they succeed in doing so, they give the credit to God and not to themselves.

Faith and Grace and Free Will (Chapters 28-30)

Next Augustine addresses the relationship between faith, grace and free will. Here he is clarifying his discussion of the "spirit of faith" in his letter to Sixtus where he said, "he would not have faith unless he received the spirit of faith" (Par. 15).

Here Augustine reaffirms his position with additional scriptural support that grace precedes faith and obedience. He differentiates between a hypothetical statement that the apostle Paul did not say "We, having the same *knowledge* of faith," with his actual statement, "We, having the spirit of faith." Augustine's argument here takes the form of "X produces Y" and "Y produces Z," therefore "X produces Y producing Z". His conclusion after tying the various Biblical verses together reads as follows, "The spirit of grace [X], therefore, causes us to have faith [Y], in order that through faith we may, on praying for it, obtain the ability to do what we are commanded [Z]" (Ch. 28).

Having drawn this conclusion, Augustine then takes up the case of prayer for unbelievers. For Augustine, praying for unbelievers is surely a case where one is asking God to act in his grace rather than relying on free will.

God's Commandments and the Fulfillment Thereof (Chapters 31-33)

"Free will…is not always good…" says Augustine, but "the grace of God is always good" (Ch. 31).

Here he replies to the Pelagian assertion that "God would not command what He knew could not be done by man" (Ch. 32). Augustine's response to this is that God commands things we cannot do in order to teach us to pray and ask for his help. He then pairs multiple statements in scripture where God commands one thing with another passage where the author is asking for God's help to do that very thing. Why, he asks, would a pious individual with the will to do what God has asked need to pray for the ability to do what he asks? He continues noting that the individual who wishes to do God's will has a good will, but a weak will (Ch. 33). But a good, weak will is not sufficient to obey God's commandments—this requires a great will, as modeled by the martyrs. The foundation of such a great will is love, which brings him to his next point.

Love and Grace (Chapters 34-40)

Moving on to the topic of love was likely not only prompted by the discussion of the "great will" in the preceding section, but also by the extended discussion in his letter to Sixtus about Jacob and Esau (Letter 194, 34-41). Augustine launches into a praise of love stringing one scriptural passage on the subject after another. He notes that Peter and John and even Jesus himself commanded us to "love one another." He returns to the same point he has made numerous times in this treatise that a commandment would be meaningless if humans did not possess free will.

Augustine then asks what the source could be for the human capacity to love God. He then sets up a mock trial between himself and the Pelagians based on this question. He lays out the stakes, noting that if the human capacity to love God is simply a matter of human free will, then the Pelagians have won their case. The Pelagians, after all, claim that love originates in human free will rather than from divine grace (Ch. 40). On the other hand, if the human capacity to love God comes directly from God, then he will have triumphed over the Pelagians. He then selects the Apostle John as the arbiter for the dispute citing 1 John 4:7 "For love is of God."

Having made this point, Augustine moves to the selection of Jesus' disciples as another example. Here he cites Jesus' words that "You have not chosen me, but I have chosen you" from John 15:16. He goes on to demonstrate that scripture after scripture affirms that Christians are not in a position to boast regarding their choice to follow God, because it is God who made the choice. Christians should instead humbly thank God that they were deemed worthy to follow God.

God Controls the Human Will (Chapters 41-43)

Augustine reiterates his main position regarding human free will; that it is never taken away, but rather, turned from bad to good, and when good, further assisted. One theme that flows throughout the letter to Sixtus is the "vessels of wrath fitted for destruction" from Romans 9:22 that he quotes multiple times. This he further explains by citing multiple cases of wicked individuals from the Old Testament, whom God used for "the praise and assistance of the good." (Ch. 41) Sometimes God has wicked people do wicked deeds for a greater good. Augustine is quick to point out here that although it is God causing them to act in specific ways, these individuals have previously acted in a manner that warrants their destruction, lest someone attempt to impugn thereby the just nature of God. In other cases, God is able to bend the will wicked people to do good deeds, when such is required. He concludes then that if God is capable of acting in the hearts of the wicked in such a manner, why should one be surprised that God may act through the Holy Spirit in his elect.

Infant Baptism and Grace (Chapters 44-45)

Whenever Augustine addresses the Pelagian controversy, he does not fail to mention the question of infant baptism.

The Pelagians vehemently denied any wrongdoing when it came to the sacrament of baptism regarding infants. Augustine quotes Pelagius' book Defense of the Freedom of the Will where the latter maintains, "We hold likewise one baptism, which we aver ought to be administered to infants in the same sacramental formula as it is to adults" (On the Grace of Christ, and on Original Sin, i 35).

Furthermore, during the Synod held in Palestine in 415, the Church accused Pelagius of the belief "That infants, even if they die unbaptized, have eternal life." Pelagius' response to this charge was unequivocal, "All these statements have not been made by me, even on their own testimony, nor do I hold myself responsible for them." (On the Proceedings of Pelagius, 57) Pelagius was even more incensed by these charges when he wrote in a letter to Pope Innocent I "there are certain subjects about which some men are trying to vilify me. One of these is, that I refuse to infants the sacrament of baptism..." (On the Grace of Christ, and on Original Sin, i 32). Again in this same letter he continues, "Who indeed is so impious as to have the heart to refuse the common redemption of the human race to an infant of any age whatever?" (On the Grace of Christ, and on Original Sin, ii 20).

These statements beg the question as to why infant baptism was continually discussed in relation to Pelagianism if their beliefs on the matter were in keeping with the Catholic Church. This is where Cœlestius' Written Statement of Belief can shed some light on the matter. Cœlestius included the following comments in his Written Statement of Belief that he presented to Pope Zosimus in A.D. 417, "[I maintain] that original sin binds no single infant. That infants, however, ought to be baptized for the remission of sins..." (On the Grace of Christ, and on Original Sin, ii 5) which he then clarifies by saying, "That infants, however, must be baptized for the remission of sins, was not admitted by us with the view of our seeming to affirm sin by transmission" (On the Grace of Christ, and on Original Sin, ii 6). Here was the real rub for Augustine. He believed that this view espoused clearly by Cœlestius undermined the basis and foundation for infant baptism even though they continued to maintain and affirm its practice. Augustine certainly cites the Pelagians as if they did not hold the practice of baptism as necessary for the salvation of infants. In his letter to Sixtus, he says "let these objectors observe how illusory is their promise that infants who die without baptism will not suffer damnation" (Letter 194, 42).

It is, therefore, no surprise that he touched on this issue at great length at the close of his letter to Sixtus (194, 31-46). The great discrepancy in the amount of space that Augustine allotted to this topic in his letter to Sixtus, which consisted of some 15 paragraphs compared with the minimal treatment (only two paragraphs) that Augustine gives this issue with the monks of Adrumetum, likely relates to the different roles played by his addressees. Sixtus was a priest in Rome, who would become Pope 14 years after Augustine wrote this letter (194) to him. As a priest, performing infant baptisms and the associated questions from parishioners about their significance and purpose would be a regular occurrence. Augustine's concern regarding Sixtus' view of infant baptism was thus quite high. For the monks in Adrumetum, on the other hand, the question of infant baptism was more of a theoretical concern. In their monastic lifestyle they themselves would have no children in need of baptism, nor would they perform baptism for parishioners in the way that Sixtus would as a priest. It should not be surprising then that Augustine passes over this issue with very minimal discussion in his treatise addressed to these monks.

When he does bring it up, he interjects a picture for the monks, taken directly from his years of experience as a priest and a bishop of a crying, squirming baby receiving the sacrament of baptism. He notes that in such a case it would certainly appear to any observer that the baby clearly does not want the sacrament. Observers freely acknowledge this fact, but it does not concern them because they observe the baby expressing dislike and distaste for many daily activities that benefit the baby. This baby, then, who has beneficial activities performed on his or her behalf, is for Augustine a perfect picture of the adult who, by means of the grace given by God the Father, is able to act uprightly.

He then anticipates the argument that pious parents beget pious infants, so that infant baptism would not be efficacious for the remission of sins, but rather symbolic of inherited state of righteousness. Augustine objects to this logic noting that occasionally pious parents adopt the children of unbelievers, or in other cases, believing parents have been unable to baptize their children before their untimely death. The reason for this seemingly arbitrary situation is attributed by him to the mysteries or "secret providence" of God with multiple scriptural citations for support.

This leads him to highlight one of the most interesting nuanced alternations in wording within one Biblical story. In the plague narrative as depicted in Exodus, the text makes repeated reference to the hardening of Pharoah's heart. What is fascinating, however, is the subtle alternation at various points in the story as to who causes this hardening. In some cases, it is the Lord who says, "I have hardened" or "I will harden" Pharoah's heart. But at other points in the narrative, the text reads, "Pharoah hardened his heart." This alternation has been frequently noted by ancient and modern commentators alike. For Augustine, it is just one more example of the delicate balance between divine grace and human free will.

Conclusion (Chapter 46)

His conclusion to this treatise involves an exhortation to the monks at Adrumetum to study this treatise, to thank God if they are able to understand it and to pray for understanding if such is lacking. Citing extensively from the books of James and Titus, Augustine reinforces that wisdom and understanding are themselves gifts (and thus the grace) of God. He then closes with a doxology.

The Aftermath of On Grace and Free Will

After meeting with Cresconius and the two monks named Felix, Augustine asked Valentinus if he would send Florus to him at Hippo Regius. The three monks had explained that Florus was the one who started the controversy in their monastery and the one whom the disaffected monks blamed for the division among them. This move by Augustine is interesting, because by all accounts Florus is Augustine's most vociferous advocate among the monks at Adrumetum.

Augustine explains his concern regarding Florus to Valentinus in this way, "For either he does not understand my book, or else, perhaps, he is himself misunderstood, when he endeavours to solve and explain a question which is a very difficult one, and intelligible to few" (Letter 214, 6).

Valentinus complied with this request and Florus arrived in Hippo Regius with a letter from Valentinus (216). Florus reported that most of the monks were pleased by Augustine's lengthy explanation of his position. One of the monks, however, remained unconvinced replying that he should not be rebuked for non-compliance with the divine commandments, but those who would otherwise rebuke him should instead pray that God might give him the grace to obey.

This obstinate monk elicited yet another lengthy treatise from the pen of Augustine, On Rebuke and Grace. With this, Augustine seems to have quieted the disturbance among the monks at Adrumetum that his letter to Sixtus (194) had aroused.

On Grace and Free Will

Chapter 1 — The Occasion and Argument of This Work.

With reference to those persons who so preach and defend man's free will, as boldly to deny, and endeavour to do away with, the grace of God which calls us to Him, and delivers us from our evil deserts, and by which we obtain the good deserts which lead to everlasting life: we have already said a good deal in discussion, and committed it to writing, so far as the Lord has vouchsafed to enable us. But since there are some persons who so defend God's grace as to deny man's free will, or who suppose that free will is denied when grace is defended, I have determined to write somewhat on this point to your Love, my brother Valentinus, and the rest of you, who are serving God together under the impulse of a mutual love. For it has been told me concerning you, brethren, by some members of your brotherhood who have visited us, and are the bearers of this communication of ours to you, that there are dissensions among you on this subject. This, then, being the case, dearly beloved, that you be not disturbed by the obscurity of this question, I counsel you first to thank God for such things as you understand; but as for all which is beyond the reach of your mind, pray for understanding from the Lord, observing, at the same time peace and love among yourselves; and until He Himself lead you to perceive what at present is beyond your comprehension, walk firmly on the ground of which you are sure. This is the advice of the Apostle Paul, who, after saying that he was not yet perfect, Philippians 3:12 a little later adds, Let us, therefore, as many as are perfect, be thus minded, Philippians 3:15 — meaning perfect to a certain extent, but not having attained to a perfection sufficient for us; and then immediately adds, And if, in any thing, you be otherwise minded, God shall reveal even this unto you. Nevertheless, whereunto we have already attained, let us walk by the same rule. Philippians 3:16 For by walking in what we have attained, we shall be able to advance to what we have not yet attained—God revealing it to us if in anything we are otherwise minded—provided we do not give up what He has already revealed.

Chapter 2 — He Proves the Existence of Free Will in Man from the Precepts Addressed to Him by God.

Now He has revealed to us, through His Holy Scriptures, that there is in a man a free choice of will. But how He has revealed this I do not recount in human language, but in divine. There is, to begin with, the fact that God's precepts themselves would be of no use to a man unless he had free choice of will, so that by performing them he might obtain the promised rewards. For they are given that no one might be able to plead the excuse of ignorance, as the Lord says concerning the Jews in the gospel: If I had not come and spoken unto them, they would not have sin; but now they have no excuse for their sin. John 15:22 Of what sin does He speak but of that great one which He foreknew, while speaking thus, that they would make their own— that is, the death they were going to inflict upon Him? For they did not have no sin before Christ came to them in the flesh. The apostle also says: The wrath of God is revealed from heaven against all ungodliness and unrighteousness of men who hold back the truth in unrighteousness; because that which may be known of God is manifest in them; for God has showed it unto them. For the invisible things of Him are from the creation of the world clearly seen— being understood by the things that are made— even His eternal power and Godhead, so that they are inexcusable. Romans 1:18-20 In what sense does he pronounce them to be inexcusable, except with reference to such excuse as human pride is apt to allege in such words as, If I had only known, I would have done it; did I not fail to do it because I was ignorant of it? or, I would do it if I knew how; but I do not know, therefore I do not do it? All such excuse is removed from them when the precept is given them, or the knowledge is made manifest to them how to avoid sin.

Chapter 3.— Sinners are Convicted When Attempting to Excuse Themselves by Blaming God, Because They Have Free Will.

There are, however, persons who attempt to find excuse for themselves even from God. The Apostle James says to such: Let no man say when he is tempted, I am tempted of God; for God cannot be tempted with evil, neither tempts He any man. But every man is tempted when he is drawn away of his own lust, and enticed. Then, when lust has conceived, it brings forth sin: and sin, when it is finished, brings forth death. James 1:13-15 Solomon, too, in his book of Proverbs, has this answer for such as wish to find an excuse for themselves from God Himself: The folly of a man spoils his ways; but he blames God in his heart. Proverbs 19:3 And in the book of

Ecclesiasticus we read: Say not, It is through the Lord that I fell away; for you ought not to do the things that He hates: nor say, He has caused me to err; for He has no need of the sinful man. The Lord hates all abomination, and they that fear God love it not. He Himself made man from the beginning, and left him in the hand of His counsel. If you be willing, you shall keep His commandments, and perform true fidelity. He has set fire and water before you: stretch forth your hand unto whether you will. Before man is life and death, and whichsoever pleases him shall be given to him. Sirach 15:11-17 Observe how very plainly is set before our view the free choice of the human will.

Chapter 4.— The Divine Commands Which are Most Suited to the Will Itself Illustrate Its Freedom.

What is the import of the fact that in so many passages God requires all His commandments to be kept and fulfilled? How does He make this requisition, if there is no free will? What means the happy man, of whom the Psalmist says that his will has been the law of the Lord? Does he not clearly enough show that a man by his own will takes his stand in the law of God? Then again, there are so many commandments which in some way are expressly adapted to the human will; for instance, there is, Be not overcome of evil, Romans 12:1 and others of similar import, such as, Be not like a horse or a mule, which have no understanding; and, Reject not the counsels of your mother; Proverbs 1:8 and, Be not wise in your own conceit; Proverbs 3:7 and, Despise not the chastening of the Lord; Proverbs 3:11 and, Forget not my law; Proverbs 3:1 and, Forbear not to do good to the poor; Proverbs 3:27 and, Devise not evil against your friend; Proverbs 3:29 and, Give no heed to a worthless woman; Proverbs 5:2 and, He is not inclined to understand how to do good; and, They refused to attend to my counsel; Proverbs 1:30 with numberless other passages of the inspired Scriptures of the Old Testament. And what do they all show us but the free choice of the human will? So, again, in the evangelical and apostolic books of the New Testament what other lesson is taught us? As when it is said, Lay not up for yourselves treasures upon earth; Matthew 6:19 and, Fear not them which kill the body; Matthew 10:28 and, If any man will come after me, let him deny himself; Matthew 16:24 and again, Peace on earth to men of good will. Luke 2:14 So also that the Apostle Paul says: Let him do what he wills;

he sins not if he marry. Nevertheless, he that stands steadfast in his heart, having no necessity, but has power over his own will, and has so decreed in his heart that he will keep his virgin, does well. 1 Corinthians 7:36-37 And so again, If I do this willingly, I have a reward; 1 Corinthians 9:17 while in another passage he says, Be sober and righteous, and sin not; 1 Corinthians 15:34 and again, As you have a readiness to will, so also let there be a prompt performance; 2 Corinthians 8:11 then he remarks to Timothy about the younger widows, When they have begun to wax wanton against Christ, they choose to marry. So in another passage, All that will to live godly in Christ Jesus shall suffer persecution; 2 Timothy 3:12 while to Timothy himself he says, Neglect not the gift that is in you. 1 Timothy 4:14 Then to Philemon he addresses this explanation: That your benefit should not be as it were of necessity, but of your own will. Servants also he advises to obey their masters with a good will. Ephesians 6:7 In strict accordance with this, James says: Do not err, my beloved brethren . . . and have not the faith of our Lord Jesus Christ with respect to persons; and, Do not speak evil one of another. James 4:11 So also John in his Epistle writes, Do not love the world, 1 John 2:15 and other things of the same import. Now wherever it is said, Do not do this, and Do not do that, and wherever there is any requirement in the divine admonitions for the work of the will to do anything, or to refrain from doing anything, there is at once a sufficient proof of free will. No man, therefore, when he sins, can in his heart blame God for it, but every man must impute the fault to himself. Nor does it detract at all from a man's own will when he performs any act in accordance with God. Indeed, a work is then to be pronounced a good one when a person does it willingly; then, too, may the reward of a good work be hoped for from Him concerning whom it is written, He shall reward every man according to his works. Matthew 16:27

Chapter 5.— He Shows that Ignorance Affords No Such Excuse as Shall Free the Offender from Punishment; But that to Sin with Knowledge is a Graver Thing Than to Sin in Ignorance.

The excuse such as men are in the habit of alleging from ignorance is taken away from those persons who know God's commandments. But neither will those be without punishment who know not the law of God. For as many as have sinned without law shall also perish without law; and as many as have sinned in the law shall be judged by the law. Romans 2:12 Now the apostle does not appear to me to have said this as if he meant that they would have to suffer something worse who in their sins are ignorant of the law than they who know it. [III.] It is seemingly worse, no doubt, to perish than to be judged; but inasmuch as he was speaking of the Gentiles and of the Jews when he used these words, because the former were without the law, but the latter had received the law, who can venture to say that the Jews who sin in the law will not perish, since they refused to believe in Christ, when it was of them that the apostle said, They shall be judged by the law? For without faith in Christ no man can be delivered; and therefore they will be so judged that they perish. If, indeed, the condition of those who are ignorant of the law of God is worse than the condition of those who know it, how can that be true which the Lord says in the gospel: The servant who knows not his lord's will, and commits things worthy of stripes, shall be beaten with few stripes; whereas the servant who knows his lord's will, and commits things worthy of stripes, shall be beaten with many stripes? Luke 12:47-48 Observe how clearly He here shows that it is a graver matter for a man to sin with knowledge than in ignorance. And yet we must not on this account betake ourselves for refuge to the shades of ignorance, with the view of finding our excuse therein. It is one thing to be ignorant, and another thing to be unwilling to know. For the will is at fault in the case of the man of whom it is said, He is not inclined to understand, so as to do good. But even the ignorance, which is not theirs who refuse to know, but theirs who are, as it were, simply ignorant, does not so far excuse any one as to exempt him from the punishment of eternal fire, though his failure to believe has been the result of his not having at all heard what he should believe; but probably only so far as to mitigate his punishment. For it was not said without reason: Pour out Your wrath upon the heathen that have not known You; nor again according to what the apostle says: When He shall come from heaven in a flame of fire to take vengeance on them that know not God. 2 Thessalonians 1:7-8 But yet in order that we may have that knowledge that will prevent our saying, each one of us, I did not know, I did not hear, I did not understand; the human will is summoned, in such words as these: Wish not to be as the horse or as the mule, which have no understanding; although it may show itself even worse, of which it is written, A stubborn servant will not be reproved by words; for even if he understand, yet he will not obey. Proverbs 29:19 But when a man says, I cannot do what I am commanded, because I am mastered by my concupiscence, he has no longer any excuse to plead from ignorance, nor reason to blame God in his heart, but he recognises and laments his own evil in himself; and still to such an one the apostle says: Be not overcome by evil, but overcome evil with good; Romans 12:21 and of course the very fact that the injunction, Consent not to be overcome, is addressed to him, undoubtedly summons the determination of his will. For to consent and to refuse are functions proper to will.

Chapter 6 — God's Grace to Be Maintained Against the Pelagians; The Pelagian Heresy Not an Old One.

It is, however, to be feared lest all these and similar testimonies of Holy Scripture (and undoubtedly there are a great many of them), in the maintenance of free will, be understood in such a way as to leave no room for God's assistance and grace in leading a godly life and a good conversation, to which the eternal reward is due; and lest poor wretched man, when he leads a good life and performs good works (or rather thinks that he leads a good life and performs good works), should dare to glory in himself and not in the Lord, and to put his hope of righteous living in himself alone; so as to be followed by the prophet Jeremiah's malediction when he says, Cursed is the man who has hope in man, and makes strong the flesh of his arm, and whose heart departs from the Lord. Jeremiah 17:5 Understand, my brethren, I pray you, this passage of the prophet. Because the prophet did not say, Cursed is the man who has hope in his own self, it might seem to some that the passage, Cursed is the man who has hope in man, was spoken to prevent man having hope in any other man but himself. In order, therefore, to show that his admonition to man was not to have hope in himself, after saying, Cursed is the man who has hope in man, he immediately added, And makes strong the flesh of his arm. He used the word arm to designate power in operation. By the term flesh, however, must be understood human frailty. And therefore he makes strong the flesh of his arm who supposes that a power which is frail and weak (that is, human) is sufficient for him to perform good works, and therefore puts not his hope in God for help. This is the reason why he subjoined the further clause, And whose heart departs from the Lord. Of this character is the Pelagian heresy, which is not an ancient one, but has only lately come into existence. Against this system of error there was first a good deal of discussion; then, as the ultimate resource, it was referred to sundry episcopal councils, the proceedings of which, not, indeed, in every instance, but in some, I have dispatched to you for your perusal. In order, then, to our performance of good works, let us not have hope in man, making strong the flesh of our arm; nor let our heart ever depart from the Lord, but let it say to him, Be Thou my helper; forsake me not, nor despise me, O God of my salvation.

Chapter 7.— Grace is Necessary Along with Free Will to Lead a Good Life.

Therefore, my dearly beloved, as we have now proved by our former testimonies from Holy Scripture that there is in man a free determination of will for living rightly and acting rightly; so now let us see what are the divine testimonies concerning the grace of God, without which we are not able to do any good thing. And first of all, I will say something about the very profession which you make in your brotherhood. Now your society, in which you are leading lives of continence, could not hold together unless you despised conjugal pleasure. Well, the Lord was one day conversing on this very topic, when His disciples remarked to Him, If such be the case of a man with his wife, it is not good to marry. He then answered them, All men cannot receive this saying, save they to whom it is given. Matthew 19:10 And was it not to Timothy's free will that the apostle appealed, when he exhorted him in these words: Keep yourself continent? 1 Timothy 5:22 He also explained the power of the will in this matter when He said, Having no necessity, but possessing power over his own will, to keep his virgin. 1 Corinthians 7:37 And yet all men do not receive this saying, except those to whom the power is given. Now they to whom this is not given either are unwilling or do not fulfil what they will; whereas they to whom it is given so will as to accomplish what they will. In order, therefore, that this saying, which is not received by all men, may yet be received by some, there are both the gift of God and free will.

Chapter 8.— Conjugal Chastity is Itself the Gift of God.

It is concerning conjugal chastity itself that the apostle treats, when he says, Let him do what he will, he sins not if he marry; 1 Corinthians

7:36 and yet this too is God's gift, for the Scripture says, It is by the Lord that the woman is joined to her husband. Accordingly the teacher of the Gentiles, in one of his discourses, commends both conjugal chastity, whereby adulteries are prevented, and the still more perfect continence which foregoes all cohabitation, and shows how both one and the other are severally the gift of God. Writing to the Corinthians, he admonished married persons not to defraud each other; and then, after his admonition to these, he added: But I could wish that all men were even as I am myself, 1 Corinthians 7:7 — meaning, of course, that he abstained from all cohabitation; and then proceeded to say: But every man has his own gift of God, one after this manner, and another after that. 1 Corinthians 7:7 Now, do the many precepts which are written in the law of God, forbidding all fornication and adultery, indicate anything else than free will? Surely such precepts would not be given unless a man had a will of his own, wherewith to obey the divine commandments. And yet it is God's gift which is indispensable for the observance of the precepts of chastity. Accordingly, it is said in the Book of Wisdom: When I knew that no one could be continent, except God gives it, then this became a point of wisdom to know whose gift it was. Wisdom 8:21 Every man, however, is tempted when he is drawn away of his own lust, and enticed James 1:14 not to observe and keep these holy precepts of chastity. If he should say in respect of these commandments, I wish to keep them, but am mastered by my concupiscence, then the Scripture responds to his free will, as I have already said: Be not overcome of evil, but overcome evil with good. Romans 12:21 In order, however, that this victory may be gained, grace renders its help; and were not this help given, then the law would be nothing but the strength of sin. For concupiscence is increased and receives greater energies from the prohibition of the law, unless the spirit of grace helps. This explains the statement of the great Teacher of the Gentiles, when he says, The sting of death is sin, and the strength of sin is the law. 1 Corinthians 15:56 See, then, I pray you, whence originates this confession of weakness, when a man says, I desire to keep what the law commands, but am overcome by the strength of my concupiscence. And when his will is addressed, and it is said, Be not overcome of evil, of what avail is anything but the succour of God's grace to the accomplishment of the precept? This the apostle himself afterwards stated; for after saying The strength of sin is the law, he immediately subjoined, But thanks be to God, who gives us the victory, through our Lord Jesus Christ. 1 Corinthians 15:57 It follows, then, that the victory in which sin is vanquished is nothing else than the gift of God, who in this contest helps free will.

Chapter 9.— Entering into Temptation. Prayer is a Proof of Grace.

Wherefore, our Heavenly Master also says: Watch and pray, that you enter not into temptation. Matthew 26:41 Let every man, therefore, when fighting against his own concupiscence, pray that he enter not into temptation; that is, that he be not drawn aside and enticed by it. But he does not enter into temptation if he conquers his evil concupiscence by good will. And yet the determination of the human will is insufficient, unless the Lord grant it victory in answer to prayer that it enter not into temptation. What, indeed, affords clearer evidence of the grace of God than the acceptance of prayer in any petition? If our Saviour had only said, Watch that you enter not into temptation, He would appear to have done nothing further than admonish man's will; but since He added the words, and pray, He showed that God helps us not to enter into temptation. It is to the free will of man that the words are addressed: My son, remove not yourself from the chastening of the Lord. Proverbs 3:11 And the Lord said: I have prayed for you, Peter, that your faith fail not. Luke 22:32 So that a man is assisted by grace, in order that his will may not be uselessly commanded.

Chapter 10 — Free Will and God's Grace are Simultaneously Commended.

When God says, Turn ye unto me, and I will turn unto you, Zechariah 1:3 one of these clauses— that which invites our return to God— evidently belongs to our will; while the other, which promises His return to us, belongs to His grace. Here, possibly, the Pelagians think they have a justification for their opinion which they so prominently advance, that God's grace is given according to our merits. In the East, indeed, that is to say, in the province of Palestine, in which is the city of Jerusalem, Pelagius, when examined in person by the bishop, did not venture to affirm this. For it happened that among the objections which were brought up against him, this in particular was objected, that he maintained that the grace of God was given according to our merits,— an opinion which was so diverse from catholic doctrine, and so hostile to the grace of Christ, that unless he had anathematized it, as laid to his charge, he himself must have been anathematized on its account. He pronounced, indeed, the required anathema upon the dogma, but how insincerely his later books plainly show; for in them he maintains absolutely no other opinion than that the grace of God is given according to our merits. Such passages do they collect out of the Scriptures—like the one which I just now quoted, Turn ye unto me, and I will turn unto you,— as if it were owing to the merit of our turning to God that His grace were given us, wherein He Himself even turns unto us. Now the persons who hold this opinion fail to observe that, unless our turning to God were itself God's gift, it would not be said to Him in prayer, Turn us again, O God of hosts; and, You, O God, wilt turn and quicken us; and again, Turn us, O God of our salvation, — with other passages of similar import, too numerous to mention here. For, with respect to our coming unto Christ, what else does it mean than our being turned to Him by believing? And yet He says: No man can come unto me, except it were given unto him of my Father. John 6:65

Chapter 11.— Other Passages of Scripture Which the Pelagians Abuse.

Then, again, there is the Scripture contained in the second book of the Chronicles: The Lord is with you when you are with Him: and if you shall seek Him you shall find Him; but if you forsake Him, He also will forsake you. 2 Chronicles 15:2 This passage, no doubt, clearly manifests the choice of the will. But they who maintain that God's grace is given according to our merits, receive these testimonies of Scripture in such a manner as to believe that our merit lies in the circumstance of our being with God, while His grace is given according to this merit, so that He too may be with us. In like manner, that our merit lies in the fact of our seeking God, and then His grace is given according to this merit, in order that we may find Him. Again, there is a passage in the first book of the same Chronicles which declares the choice of the will: And you, Solomon, my son, know the God of your father, and serve Him with a perfect heart and with a willing mind, for the Lord searches all hearts, and understands all the imaginations of the thoughts; if you seek Him, He will be found of you; but if you forsake

Him, He will cast you off for ever. 1 Chronicles 28:9 But these people find some room for human merit in the clause, If you seek Him, and then the grace is thought to be given according to this merit in what is said in the ensuing words, He will be found of you. And so they labour with all their might to show that God's grace is given according to our merits,— in other words, that grace is not grace. For, as the apostle most expressly says, to them who receive reward according to merit the recompense is not reckoned of grace but of debt. Romans 4:4

Chapter 12.— He Proves Out of St. Paul that Grace is Not Given According to Men's Merits.

Now there was, no doubt, a decided merit in the Apostle Paul, but it was an evil one, while he persecuted the Church, and he says of it: I am not meet to be called an apostle, because I persecuted the Church of God. 1 Corinthians 15:9 And it was while he had this evil merit that a good one was rendered to him instead of the evil; and, therefore, he went on at once to say, But by the grace of God I am what I am. 1 Corinthians 15:10 Then, in order to exhibit also his free will, he added in the next clause, And His grace within me was not in vain, but I have laboured more abundantly than they all. This free will of man he appeals to in the case of others also, as when he says to them, We beseech you that you receive not the grace of God in vain. 2 Corinthians 6:1 Now, how could he so enjoin them, if they received God's grace in such a manner as to lose their own will? Nevertheless, lest the will itself should be deemed capable of doing any good thing without the grace of God, after saying, His grace within me was not in vain, but I have laboured more abundantly than they all, he immediately added the qualifying clause, Yet not I, but the grace of God which was with me. 1 Corinthians 15:10 In other words, Not I alone, but the grace of God with me. And thus, neither was it the grace of God alone, nor was it he himself alone, but it was the grace of God with him. For his call, however, from heaven and his conversion by that great and most effectual call, God's grace was alone, because his merits, though great, were yet evil. Then, to quote one passage more, he says to Timothy: But be a co-labourer with the gospel, according to the power of God, who saves us and calls us with His holy calling—not according to our works but according to His own purpose and grace, which was given us in Christ Jesus. 2 Timothy 1:8-9 Then, elsewhere, he enumerates his merits, and gives us this description of their evil character: For we ourselves also were formerly foolish, unbelieving, deceived, serving various lusts and pleasures, living in malice and envy, hateful, and hating one another. Titus 3:3 Nothing, to be sure, but punishment was due to such a course of evil desert! God, however, who returns good for evil by His grace, which is not given according to our merits, enabled the apostle to conclude his statement and say: But when the kindness and love of our Saviour God shone upon us—not of works of righteousness which we have done, but according to His mercy He saved us, by the laver of regeneration and renewal of the Holy Ghost, whom He shed upon us abundantly through Jesus Christ our Saviour; that, being justified by His grace, we should be made heirs according to the hope of eternal life. Titus 3:4-7

Chapter 13 — The Grace of God is Not Given According to Merit, But Itself Makes All Good Desert.

From these and similar passages of Scripture, we gather the proof that God's grace is not given according to our merits. The truth is, we see that it is given not only where there are no good, but even where there are many evil merits preceding: and we see it so given daily. But it is plain that when it has been given, also our good merits begin to be— yet only by means of it; for, were that only to withdraw itself, man falls, not raised up, but precipitated by free will. Wherefore no man ought, even when he begins to possess good merits, to attribute them to himself, but to God, who is thus addressed by the Psalmist: Be Thou my helper, forsake me not. By saying, Forsake me not, he shows that if he were to be forsaken, he is unable of himself to do any good thing. Wherefore also he says: I said in my abundance, I shall never be moved, for he thought that he had such an abundance of good to call his own that he would not be moved. But in order that he might be taught whose that was, of which he had begun to boast as if it were his own, he was admonished by the gradual desertion of God's grace, and says: O Lord, in Your good pleasure You added strength to my beauty. Thou did, however, turn away Your face, and then I was troubled and distressed. Thus, it is necessary for a man that he should be not only justified when unrighteous by the grace of God—that is, be changed from unholiness to righteousness—when he is requited with good for his evil; but that, even after he has become justified by faith, grace should accompany him on his way, and he should lean upon it, lest he fall. On this account it is written concerning the Church herself in the book of Canticles: Who is this that comes up in white raiment, leaning upon her kinsman? Song of Songs 8:5 Made white is she who by herself alone could not be white. And by whom has she been made white except by Him who says by the prophet, Though your sins be as purple, I will make them white as snow? Isaiah 1:18 At the time, then, that she was made white, she deserved nothing good; but now that she is made white, she walks well—but it is only by her continuing ever to lean upon Him by whom she was made white. Wherefore, Jesus Himself, on whom she leans that was made white, said to His disciples, Without me you can do nothing. John 15:5

Chapter 14.— Paul First Received Grace that He Might Win the Crown.

Let us return now to the Apostle Paul, who, as we have found, obtained God's grace, who recompenses good for evil, without any good merits of his own, but rather with many evil merits. Let us see what he says when his final sufferings were approaching, writing to Timothy: I am now ready to be offered, and the time of my departure is at hand. I have fought a good fight; I have finished my course; I have kept the faith. 2 Timothy 4:6-7 He enumerates these as, of course, now his good merits; so that, as after his evil merits he obtained grace, so now, after his good merits, he might receive the crown. Observe, therefore, what follows: There is henceforth laid up for me, he says, a crown of righteousness, which the Lord, the righteous Judge, shall give me at that day. 2 Timothy 4:8 Now, to whom should the righteous Judge award the crown, except to him on whom the merciful Father had bestowed grace? And how could the crown be one of righteousness, unless the grace had preceded which justifies the ungodly? How, moreover, could these things now be awarded as of debt, unless the other had been before given as a free gift?

Chapter 15.— The Pelagians Profess that the Only Grace Which is Not Given According to Our Merits is that of the Forgiveness of Sins.

When, however, the Pelagians say that the only grace which is not given according to our merits is that whereby his sins are forgiven to man, but that that which is given in the end, that is, eternal life, is rendered to our preceding merits: they must not be allowed to go without an answer. If, indeed, they so understand our merits as to acknowledge them, too, to be the gifts of God, then their opinion would not deserve reprobation. But inasmuch as they so preach human merits as to declare that a man has them of his own self, then most rightly the apostle replies: Who makes you to differ from another? And what have you, that you did not receive? Now, if you received it, why do you glory as if you had not received it? 1 Corinthians 4:7 To a man who holds such views, it is perfect truth to say: It is His own gifts that God crowns, not your merits,— if, at least, your merits are of your own self, not of Him. If, indeed, they are such, they are evil; and God does not crown them; but if they are good, they are God's gifts, because, as the Apostle James says, Every good gift and every perfect gift is from above, and comes down from the Father of lights. James 1:17 In accordance with which John also, the Lord's forerunner, declares: A man can receive nothing except it be given him from heaven John 3:27 — from heaven, of course, because from thence came also the Holy Ghost, when Jesus ascended up on high, led captivity captive, and gave gifts to men. If, then, your good merits are God's gifts, God does not crown your merits as your merits, but as His own gifts.

Chapter 16 — Paul Fought, But God Gave the Victory: He Ran, But God Showed Mercy.

Let us, therefore, consider those very merits of the Apostle Paul which he said the Righteous Judge would recompense with the crown of righteousness; and let us see whether these merits of his were really his own— I mean, whether they were obtained by him of himself, or were the gifts of God. I have fought, says he, the good fight; I have finished my course; I have kept the faith. 2 Timothy 4:7 Now, in the first place, these good works were nothing, unless they had been preceded by good thoughts. Observe, therefore, what he says concerning these very thoughts. His words, when writing to the Corinthians, are: Not that we are sufficient of ourselves to think anything as of ourselves; but our sufficiency is of God. 2 Corinthians 3:5 Then let us look at each several merit. I have fought the good fight. Well, now, I want to know by what power he fought. Was it by a power which he possessed of himself, or by strength given to him from above? It is impossible to suppose that so great a teacher as the apostle was ignorant of the law of God, which proclaims the following in Deuteronomy: Say not in your heart, My own strength and energy of hand has wrought for me this great power; but you shall remember the Lord your God, how it is He that gives you strength to acquire such power. Deuteronomy 8:17 And what avails the good fight, unless followed by victory? And who gives the victory but He of whom the apostle says himself, Thanks be to God, who gives us the victory through our Lord Jesus Christ? 1 Corinthians 15:57 Then, in another passage, having quoted from the Psalm these words: Because for Your sake we are killed all the day long; we are accounted as sheep for slaughter, he went on to declare: Nay, in all these things we are more than conquerors, through Him that loved us. Romans 8:37 Not by ourselves, therefore, is the victory accomplished, but by Him who has loved us. In the second clause he says, I have finished my course. Now, who is it that says this, but he who declares in another passage, So then it is not of him that wills, nor of him that runs, but of God that shows mercy. Romans 9:16 And this sentence can by no means be transposed, so that it could be said: It is not of God, who shows mercy, but of the man who wills and runs. If any person be bold enough to express the matter thus, he shows himself most plainly to be at issue with the apostle.

Chapter 17.— The Faith that He Kept Was the Free Gift of God.

His last clause runs thus: I have kept the faith. But he who says this is the same who declares in another passage, I have obtained mercy that I might be faithful. 1 Corinthians 7:25 He does not say, I obtained mercy because I was faithful, but in order that I might be faithful, thus showing that even faith itself cannot be had without God's mercy, and that it is the gift of God. This he very expressly teaches us when he says, For by grace are you saved through faith, and that not of yourselves; it is the gift of God. Ephesians 2:8 They might possibly say, We received grace because we believed; as if they would attribute the faith to themselves, and the grace to God. Therefore, the apostle having said, You are saved through faith, added, And that not of yourselves, but it is the gift of God. And again, lest they should say they deserved so great a gift by their works, he immediately added, Not of works, lest any man should boast. Ephesians 2:9 Not that he denied good works, or emptied them of their value, when he says that God renders to every man according to his works; Romans 2:6 but because works proceed from faith, and not faith from works. Therefore it is from Him that we have works of righteousness, from whom comes also faith itself, concerning which it is written, The just shall live by faith. Habakkuk 2:4

Chapter 18.— Faith Without Good Works is Not Sufficient for Salvation.

Unintelligent persons, however, with regard to the apostle's statement: We conclude that a man is justified by faith without the works of the law, Romans 3:28 have thought him to mean that faith suffices to a man, even if he lead a bad life, and has no good works. Impossible is it that such a character should be deemed a vessel of election by the apostle, who, after declaring that in Christ Jesus neither circumcision avails anything, nor uncircumcision, Galatians 5:6 adds at once, but faith which works by love. It is such faith which severs God's faithful from unclean demons—for even these believe and tremble, James 2:19 as the Apostle James says; but they do not do well. Therefore they possess not the faith by which the just man lives—the faith which works by love in such wise, that God recompenses it according to its works with eternal life. But inasmuch as we have even our good works from God, from whom likewise comes our faith and our love, therefore the selfsame great teacher of the Gentiles has designated eternal life itself as His gracious gift. Romans 6:23

Chapter 19 — How is Eternal Life Both a Reward for Service and a Free Gift of Grace?

And hence there arises no small question, which must be solved by the Lord's gift. If eternal life is rendered to good works, as the Scripture most openly declares: Then He shall reward every man according to his works: Matthew 16:27 how can eternal life be a matter of grace, seeing that grace is not rendered to works, but is given gratuitously, as the apostle himself tells us: To him that works is the reward not reckoned of grace, but of debt; Romans 4:4 and again: There is a remnant saved according to the election of grace; with these words immediately subjoined: And if of grace, then is it no more of works; otherwise grace is no more grace? Romans 11:5-6 How, then, is eternal life by grace, when it is received from works? Does the apostle perchance not say that eternal life is a grace? Nay, he has so called it, with a clearness which none can possibly gainsay. It requires no acute intellect, but only an attentive reader, to discover this. For after saying, The wages of sin is death, he at once added, The grace of God is eternal life through Jesus Christ our Lord. Romans 6:23

Chapter 20.— The Question Answered. Justification is Grace Simply and Entirely, Eternal Life is Reward and Grace.

This question, then, seems to me to be by no means capable of solution, unless we understand that even those good works of ours, which are recompensed with eternal life, belong to the grace of God, because of what is said by the Lord Jesus: Without me you can do nothing. John 15:5 And the apostle himself, after saying, By grace are you saved through faith; and that not of yourselves, it is the gift of God: not of works, lest any man should boast; Ephesians 2:8-9 saw, of course, the possibility that men would think from this statement that good works are not necessary to those who believe, but that faith alone suffices for them; and again, the possibility of men's boasting of their good works, as if they were of themselves capable of performing them. To meet, therefore, these opinions on both sides, he immediately added, For we are His workmanship, created in Christ Jesus unto good works, which God has before ordained that we should walk in them. Ephesians 2:10 What is the purport of his saying, Not of works, lest any man should boast, while commending the grace of God? And then why does he afterwards, when giving a reason for using such words, say, For we are His workmanship, created in Christ Jesus unto good works? Why, therefore, does it run, Not of works, lest any man should boast? Now, hear and understand. Not of works is spoken of the works which you suppose have their origin in yourself alone; but you have to think of works for which God has moulded (that is, has formed and created) you. For of these he says, We are His workmanship, created in Christ Jesus unto good works. Now he does not here speak of that creation which made us human beings, but of that in reference to which one said who was already in full manhood, Create in me a clean heart, O God; concerning which also the apostle says, Therefore, if any man be in Christ, he is a new creature: old things are passed away; behold, all things have become new. And all things are of God. 2 Corinthians 5:17-18 We are framed, therefore, that is, formed and created, in the good works which we have not ourselves prepared, but God has before ordained that we should walk in them. It follows, then, dearly beloved, beyond all doubt, that as your good life is nothing else than God's grace, so also the eternal life which is the recompense of a good life is the grace of God; moreover it is given gratuitously, even as that is given gratuitously to which it is given. But that to which it is given is solely and simply grace; this therefore is also that which is given to it, because it is its reward—grace is for grace, as if remuneration for righteousness; in order that it may be true, because it is true, that God shall reward every man according to his works.

Chapter 21 — Eternal Life is Grace for Grace.

Perhaps you ask whether we ever read in the Sacred Scriptures of grace for grace. Well you possess the Gospel according to John, which is perfectly clear in its very great light. Here John the Baptist says of Christ: Of His fullness have we all received, even grace for grace. John 1:16 So that out of His fullness we have received, according to our humble measure, our particles of ability as it were for leading good lives— according as God has dealt to every man his measure of faith; Romans 12:3 because every man has his proper gift of God; one after this manner, and another after that. 1 Corinthians 7:7 And this is grace. But, over and above this, we shall also receive grace for grace, when we shall have awarded to us eternal life, of which the apostle said: The grace of God is eternal life through Jesus Christ our Lord, Romans 6:23 having just said that the wages of sin is death. Deservedly did he call it wages, because everlasting death is awarded as its proper due to diabolical service. Now, when it was in his power to say, and rightly to say: But the wages of righteousness is eternal life, he yet preferred to say: The grace of God is eternal life; in order that we may hence understand that God does not, for any merits of our own, but from His own divine compassion, prolong our existence to everlasting life. Even as the Psalmist says to his soul, Who crowns you with mercy and compassion. Well, now, is not a crown given as the reward of good deeds? It is, however, only because He works good works in good men, of whom it is said, It is God which works in you both to will and to do of His good pleasure, Philippians 2:13 that the Psalm has it, as just now quoted: He crowns you with mercy and compassion, since it is through His mercy that we perform the good deeds to which the crown is awarded. It is not, however, to be for a moment supposed, because he said, It is God that works in you both to will and to do of his own good pleasure, that free will is taken away. If this, indeed, had been his meaning, he would not have said just before, Work out your own salvation with fear and trembling. Philippians 2:12 For when the command is given to work, their free will is addressed; and when it is added, with fear and trembling, they are warned against boasting of their good deeds as if they were their own, by attributing to themselves the performance of anything good. It is pretty much as if the apostle had this question put to him: Why did you use the phrase, 'with fear and trembling'? And as if he answered the inquiry of his examiners by telling them, For it is God which works in you. Because if you fear and tremble, you do not boast of your good works— as if they were your own, since it is God who works within you.

Chapter 22 — Who is the Transgressor of the Law? The Oldness of Its Letter. The Newness of Its Spirit.

Therefore, brethren, you ought by free will not do evil but do good; this, indeed, is the lesson taught us in the law of God, in the Holy Scriptures— both Old and New. Let us, however, read, and by the Lord's help understand, what the apostle tells us: Because by the deeds of the law there shall no flesh be justified in His sight; for by the law is the knowledge of sin. Romans 3:20 Observe, he says the knowledge, not the destruction, of sin. But when a man knows sin, and grace does not help him to avoid what he knows, undoubtedly the law works wrath. And this the apostle explicitly says in another passage. His words are: The law works wrath. Romans 4:15 The reason of this statement lies in the fact that God's wrath is greater in the case of the transgressor who by the law knows sin, and yet commits it; such a man is thus a transgressor of the law, even as the apostle says in another sentence, For where no law is, there is no transgression. Romans 4:15 It is in accordance with this principle that he elsewhere says, That we may serve in newness of spirit, and not in the oldness of the letter; Romans 7:6 wishing the law to be here understood by the oldness of the letter, and what else by newness of spirit than grace? Then, that it might not be thought that he had brought any accusation, or suggested any blame, against the law, he immediately takes himself to task with this inquiry: What shall we say, then? Is the law sin? God forbid. He then adds the statement: Nay, I had not known sin but by the law; Romans 7:6-7 which is of the same import as the passage above quoted: By the law is the knowledge of sin. Romans 3:20 Then: For I had not known lust, he says, except the law had said, 'You shall not covet.' Exodus 20:17 But sin, taking occasion by the commandment, wrought in me all manner of concupiscence. For without the law sin was dead. For I was alive without the law once; but when the commandment came, sin revived, and I died. And the commandment, which was ordained to life, I found to be unto death. For sin, taking occasion by the commandment, deceived me, and by it slew me. Wherefore the law is holy; and the commandment holy, just, and good. Was, then, that which is good made death unto me? God forbid. But sin, that it might appear sin, worked death in me by that which is good—in order that the sinner, or the sin, might by the commandment become beyond measure. Romans 7:7-13 And to the Galatians he writes: Knowing that a man is not justified by the works of the law, except through faith in Jesus Christ, even we have believed in Jesus Christ, that we might be justified by the faith of Christ, and not by the works of the law; for by the works of the law shall no flesh be justified. Galatians 2:16

Chapter 23 — The Pelagians Maintain that the Law is the Grace of God Which Helps Us Not to Sin.

Why, therefore, do those very vain and perverse Pelagians say that the law is the grace of God by which we are helped not to sin? Do they not, by making such an allegation, unhappily and beyond all doubt contradict the great apostle? He, indeed, says, that by the law sin received strength against man; and that man, by the commandment, although it be holy, and just, and good, nevertheless dies, and that death works in him through that which is good, from which death there is no deliverance unless the Spirit quickens him, whom the letter had killed,— as he says in another passage, The letter kills, but the Spirit gives life. 2 Corinthians 3:6 And yet these obstinate persons, blind to God's light, and deaf to His voice, maintain that the letter which kills gives life, and thus gainsay the quickening Spirit. Therefore, brethren (that I may warn you with better effect in the words of the apostle himself), we are debtors not to the flesh, to live after the flesh; for if you live after the flesh you shall die; but if you through the Spirit do mortify the deeds of the body, you shall live. Romans 8:12-13 I have said this to deter your free will from evil, and to exhort it to good by apostolic words; but yet you must not therefore glory in man—that is to say, in your own selves,— and not in the Lord, when you live not after the flesh, but through the Spirit mortify the deeds of the flesh. For in order that they to whom the apostle addressed this language might not exalt themselves, thinking that they were themselves able of their own spirit to do such good works as these, and not by the Spirit of God, after saying to them, If you through the Spirit do mortify the deeds of the flesh, you shall live, he at once added, For as many as are led by the Spirit of God, they are the sons of God. Romans 8:14 When, therefore, you by the Spirit mortify the deeds of the flesh, that you may have life, glorify Him, praise Him, give thanks to Him by whose Spirit you are so led as to be able to do such things as show you to be the children of God; for as many as are led by the Spirit of God, they are the sons of God.

Chapter 24 — Who May Be Said to Wish to Establish Their Own Righteousness. God's Righteousness, So Called, Which Man Has from God.

As many, therefore, as are led by their own spirit, trusting in their own virtue, with the addition merely of the law's assistance, without the help of grace, are not the sons of God. Such are they of whom the same apostle speaks as being ignorant of God's righteousness, and wishing to establish their own righteousness, who have not submitted themselves to the righteousness of God. Romans 10:3 He said this of the Jews, who in their self-assumption rejected grace, and therefore did not believe in Christ. Their own righteousness, indeed, he says, they wish to establish; and this righteousness is of the law,— not that the law was established by themselves, but that they had constituted their righteousness in the law which is of God, when they supposed themselves able to fulfil that law by their own strength, ignorant of God's righteousness—not indeed that by which God is Himself righteous, but that which man has from God. And that you may know that he designated as theirs the righteousness which is of the law, and as God's that which man receives from God, hear what he says in another passage, when speaking of Christ: For whose sake I counted all things not only as loss, but I deemed them to be dung, that I might win Christ, and be found in Him— not having my own righteousness, which is of the law, but that which is through the faith of Christ, which is of God. Philippians 3:8-9 Now what does he mean by not having my own righteousness, which is of the law, when the law is really not his at all, but God's,— except this, that he called it his own righteousness, although it was of the law, because he thought he could fulfil the law by his own will, without the aid of grace which is through faith in Christ? Wherefore, after saying, Not having my own righteousness, which is of the law, he immediately subjoined, But that which is through the faith of Christ, which is of God. This is what they were ignorant of, of whom he says, Being ignorant of God's righteousness,— that is, the righteousness which is of God (for it is given not by the letter, which kills, but by the life-giving Spirit), and wishing to establish their own righteousness, which he expressly described as the righteousness of the law, when he said, Not having my own righteousness, which is of the law; they were not subject to the righteousness of God—in other words, they submitted not themselves to the grace of God. For they were under the law, not under grace, and therefore sin had dominion over them, from which a man is not freed by the law, but by grace. On which account he elsewhere says, For sin shall not have dominion over you; because you are not under the law, but under grace. Romans 6:14 Not that the law is evil; but because they are under its power, whom it makes guilty by imposing commandments, not by aiding. It is by grace that any one is a doer of the law; and without this grace, he who is placed under the law will be only a hearer of the law. To such persons he addresses these words: You who are justified by the law are fallen from grace. Galatians 5:4

Chapter 25 — As The Law is Not, So Neither is Our Nature Itself that Grace by Which We are Christians.

Now who can be so insensible to the words of the apostle, who so foolishly, nay, so insanely ignorant of the purport of his statement, as to venture to affirm that the law is grace, when he who knew very well what he was saying emphatically declares, You who are justified by the law are fallen from grace? Well, but if the law is not grace, seeing that in order that the law itself may be kept, it is not the law, but only grace which can give help, will not nature at any rate be grace? For this, too, the Pelagians have been bold enough to aver, that grace is the nature in which we were created, so as to possess a rational mind, by which we are enabled to understand—formed as we are in the image of God, so as to have dominion over the fish of the sea, and over the fowl of the air, and over every living thing that creeps upon the earth. This, however, is not the grace which the apostle commends to us through the faith of Jesus Christ. For it is certain that we possess this nature in common with ungodly men and unbelievers; whereas the grace which comes through the faith of Jesus Christ belongs only to them to whom the faith itself appertains. For all men have not faith. 2 Thessalonians 3:2 Now, as the apostle, with perfect truth, says to those who by wishing to be justified by the law have fallen from grace, If righteousness come by the law, then Christ is dead in vain; Galatians 2:21 so likewise, to those who think that the grace which he commends and faith in Christ receives, is nature, the same language is with the same degree of truth applicable: if righteousness come from nature, then Christ is dead in vain. But the law was in existence up to that time, and it did not justify; and nature existed too, but it did not justify. It was not, then, in vain that Christ died, in order that the law might be fulfilled through Him who said, I have come not to destroy the law, but to fulfil it; Matthew 5:17 and that our nature, which was lost through Adam, might through Him be recovered, who said that He had come to seek and to save that which was lost; in whose coming the old fathers likewise who loved God believed.

Chapter 26.— The Pelagians Contend that the Grace, Which is Neither the Law Nor Nature, Avails Only to the Remission of Past Sins, But Not to the Avoidance of Future Ones.

They also maintain that God's grace, which is given through the faith of Jesus Christ, and which is neither the law nor nature, avails only for the remission of sins that have been committed, and not for the shunning of future ones, or the subjugation of those which are now assailing us. Now if all this were true, surely after offering the petition of the Lord's Prayer, Forgive us our debts, as we forgive our debtors, we could hardly go on and say, And lead us not into temptation. Matthew 6:12-13 The former petition we present that our sins may be forgiven; the latter, that they may be avoided or subdued—a favour which we should by no means beg of our Father who is in heaven if we were able to accomplish it by the virtue of our human will. Now I strongly advise and earnestly require your Love to read attentively the book of the blessed Cyprian which he wrote On the Lord's Prayer. As far as the Lord shall assist you, understand it, and commit it to memory. In this work you will see how he so appeals to the free will of those whom he edifies in his treatise, as to show them, that whatever they have to fulfil in the law, they must ask for in the prayer. But this, of course, would be utterly empty if the human will were sufficient for the performance without the help of God.

Chapter 27 — Grace Effects the Fulfilment of the Law, the Deliverance of Nature, and the Suppression of Sin's Dominion.

It has, however, been shown to demonstration that instead of really maintaining free will, they have only inflated a theory of it, which, having no stability, has fallen to the ground. Neither the knowledge of God's law, nor nature, nor the mere remission of sins is that grace which is given to us through our Lord Jesus Christ; but it is this very grace which accomplishes the fulfilment of the law, and the liberation of nature, and the removal of the dominion of sin. Being, therefore, convicted on these points, they resort to another expedient, and endeavour to show in some way or other that the grace of God is given us according to our merits. For they say: Granted that it is not given to us according to the merits of good works, inasmuch as it is through it that we do any good thing, still it is given to us according to the merits of a good will; for, say they, the good will of him who prays precedes his prayer, even as the will of the believer preceded his faith, so that according to these merits the grace of God who hears, follows.

Chapter 28.— Faith is the Gift of God.

I have already discussed the point concerning faith, that is, concerning the will of him who believes, even so far as to show that it appertains to grace—so that the apostle did not tell us, I have obtained mercy because I was faithful; but he said, I have obtained mercy in order to be faithful. 1 Corinthians 7:25 And there are many other passages of similar import—among them that in which he bids us think soberly, according as God has dealt out to every man the proportion of faith;

Romans 12:3 and that which I have already quoted: By grace are you saved through faith; and that not of yourselves; it is the gift of God; Ephesians 2:8 and again another in the same Epistle to the Ephesians: Peace be to the brethren, and love with faith, from God the Father, and the Lord Jesus Christ; Ephesians 6:23 and to the same effect that passage in which he says, For unto you it is given in the behalf of Christ not only to believe in Him, but also to suffer for His sake. Philippians 1:29 Both alike are therefore due to the grace of God—the faith of those who believe, and the patience of those who suffer, because the apostle spoke of both as given. Then, again, there is the passage, especially noticeable, in which he says, We, having the same spirit of faith, 2 Corinthians 4:13 for his phrase is not the knowledge of faith, but the spirit of faith; and he expressed himself thus in order that we might understand how that faith is given to us, even when it is not sought, so that other blessings may be granted to it at its request. For how, says he, shall they call upon Him in whom they have not believed? Romans 10:14 The spirit of grace, therefore, causes us to have faith, in order that through faith we may, on praying for it, obtain the ability to do what we are commanded. On this account the apostle himself constantly puts faith before the law; since we are not able to do what the law commands unless we obtain the strength to do it by the prayer of faith.

Chapter 29.— God is Able to Convert Opposing Wills, and to Take Away from the Heart Its Hardness.

Now if faith is simply of free will, and is not given by God, why do we pray for those who will not believe, that they may believe? This it would be absolutely useless to do, unless we believe, with perfect propriety, that Almighty God is able to turn to belief wills that are perverse and opposed to faith. Man's free will is addressed when it is said, Today, if you will hear His voice, harden not your hearts. But if God were not able to remove from the human heart even its obstinacy and hardness, He would not say, through the prophet, I will take from them their heart of stone, and will give them a heart of flesh. Ezekiel 11:19 That all this was foretold in reference to the New Testament is shown clearly enough by the apostle when he says, You are our epistle, . . . written not with ink, but with the Spirit of the living God; not in tables of stone, but in fleshly tables of the heart. 2 Corinthians 3:2-3

We must not, of course, suppose that such a phrase as this is used as if those might live in a fleshly way who ought to live spiritually; but inasmuch as a stone has no feeling, with which man's hard heart is compared, what was there left Him to compare man's intelligent heart with but the flesh, which possesses feeling? For this is what is said by the prophet Ezekiel: I will give them another heart, and I will put a new spirit within you; and I will take the stony heart out of their flesh, and will give them a heart of flesh; that they may walk in my statutes, and keep mine ordinances, and do them: and they shall be my people, and I will be their God, says the Lord. Ezekiel 11:19-20 Now can we possibly, without extreme absurdity, maintain that there previously existed in any man the good merit of a good will, to entitle him to the removal of his stony heart, when all the while this very heart of stone signifies nothing else than a will of the hardest kind and such as is absolutely inflexible against God? For where a good will precedes, there is, of course, no longer a heart of stone.

Chapter 30.— The Grace by Which the Stony Heart is Removed is Not Preceded by Good Deserts, But by Evil Ones.

In another passage, also, by the same prophet, God, in the clearest language, shows us that it is not owing to any good merits on the part of men, but for His own name's sake, that He does these things. This is His language: This I do, O house of Israel, but for mine holy name's sake, which you have profaned among the heathen, whither ye went. And I will sanctify my great name, which was profaned among the heathen, which you have profaned in the midst of them; and the heathen shall know that I am the Lord, says the Lord God, when I shall be sanctified in you before their eyes. For I will take you from among the heathen, and gather you out of all countries, and will bring you into your own land. Then will I sprinkle you with clean water, and you shall be clean: from all your own filthiness, and from all your idols will I cleanse you. A new heart also will I give you, and a new spirit will I put within you; and the stony heart shall be taken away out of your flesh, and I will give you a heart of flesh. And I will put my Spirit within you, and will cause you to walk in my statutes, and you shall keep my judgments, and do them. Ezekiel 36:22-27 Now who is so blind as not to see, and who so stone-like as not to feel, that this grace is not given according to the merits of a good will, when the Lord declares and testifies, It is I, O house of Israel, who do this, but for my holy name's sake? Now why did He say It is I that do it, but for my holy name's sake, were it not that they should not think that it was owing to their own good merits that these things were happening, as the Pelagians hesitate not unblushingly to say? But there were not only no good merits of theirs, but the Lord shows that evil ones actually preceded; for He says, But for my holy name's sake, which you have profaned among the heathen. Who can fail to observe how dreadful is the evil of profaning the Lord's own holy name? And yet, for the sake of this very name of mine, says He, which you have profaned, I, even I, will make you good, but not for your own sakes; and, as He adds, I will sanctify my great name, which was profaned among the heathen, which you have profaned in the midst of them. He says that He sanctifies His name, which He had already declared to be holy. Therefore, this is just what we pray for in the Lord's Prayer— Hallowed be Your name. We ask for the hallowing among men of that which is in itself undoubtedly always holy. Then it follows, And the heathen shall know that I am the Lord, says the Lord God, when I shall be sanctified in you. Although, then, He is Himself always holy, He is, nevertheless, sanctified in those on whom He bestows His grace, by taking from them that stony heart by which they profaned the name of the Lord.

Chapter 31 — Free Will Has Its Function in the Heart's Conversion; But Grace Too Has Its.

Lest, however, it should be thought that men themselves in this matter do nothing by free will, it is said in the Psalm, Harden not your hearts; and in Ezekiel himself, Cast away from you all your transgressions, which you have impiously committed against me; and make you a new heart and a new spirit; and keep all my commandments. For why will you die, O house of Israel, says the Lord? For I have no pleasure in the death of him that dies, says the Lord God: and turn ye, and live. Ezekiel 18:31-32 We should remember that it is He who says, Turn ye and live, to whom it is said in prayer, Turn us again, O God. We should remember that He says, Cast away from you all your transgressions, when it is even He who justifies the ungodly. We should remember that He says, Make you a new heart and a new spirit, who also promises, I will give you a new heart, and a new spirit will I put within you. Ezekiel 36:26 How is it, then, that He who says, Make you, also says, I will give you? Why does He command, if He is to give? Why does He give if man is to make, except it be that He gives what He commands when He helps him to obey whom He commands? There is, however, always within us a free will—but it is not always good; for it is either free from righteousness when it serves sin—and then it is evil—or else it is free from sin when it serves righteousness—and then it is good. But the grace of God is always good; and by it it comes to pass that a man is of a good will, though he was before of an evil one. By it also it comes to pass that the very good will, which has now begun to be, is enlarged, and made so great that it is able to fulfil the divine commandments which it shall wish, when it shall once firmly and perfectly wish. This is the purport of what the Scripture says: If you will, you shall keep the commandments; Sirach 15:15 so that the man who wills but is not able knows that he does not yet fully will, and prays that he may have so great a will that it may suffice for keeping the commandments. And thus, indeed, he receives assistance to perform what he is commanded. Then is the will of use when we have ability; just as ability is also then of use when we have the will. For what does it profit us if we will what we are unable to do, or else do not will what we are able to do?

Chapter 32 — In What Sense It is Rightly Said That, If We Like, We May Keep God's Commandments.

The Pelagians think that they know something great when they assert that God would not command what He knew could not be done by man. Who can be ignorant of this? But God commands some things which we cannot do, in order that we may know what we ought to ask of Him. For this is faith itself, which obtains by prayer what the law commands. He, indeed, who said, If you will, you shall keep the commandments, did in the same book of Ecclesiasticus afterwards say, Who shall give a watch before my mouth, and a seal of wisdom upon my lips, that I fall not suddenly thereby, and that my tongue destroy me not. Sirach 22:27 Now he had certainly heard and received these commandments: Keep your tongue from evil, and your lips from speaking guile. Forasmuch, then, as what he said is true: If you will, you shall keep the commandments, why does he want a watch to be given before his mouth, like him who says in the Psalm, Set a watch, O Lord, before my mouth? Why is he not satisfied with God's commandment and his own will; since, if he has the will, he shall keep the commandments? How many of God's commandments are directed against pride! He is quite aware of them; if he will, he may keep them. Why, therefore, does he shortly afterwards say, O God, Father and God of my life, give me not a proud look? Sirach 23:4 The law had long ago said to him, You shall not covet; Exodus 20:17 let him then only will, and do what he is bidden, because, if he has the will, he shall keep the commandments. Why, therefore, does he afterwards say, Turn away from me concupiscence? Sirach 23:5 Against luxury, too, how many commandments has God enjoined! Let a man observe them; because, if he will, he may keep the commandments. But what means that cry to God, Let not the greediness of the belly nor lust of the flesh take hold on me!? Sirach 23:6 Now, if we were to put this question to him personally, he would very rightly answer us and say, From that prayer of mine, in which I offer this particular petition to God, you may understand in what sense I said, If you will, you may keep the commandments. For it is certain that we keep the commandments if we will; but because the will is prepared by the Lord, we must ask of Him for such a force of will as suffices to make us act by the willing. It is certain that it is we that will when we will, but it is He who makes us will what is good, of whom it is said (as he has just now expressed it), The will is prepared by the Lord. Proverbs 8:35 Of the same Lord it is said, The steps of a man are ordered by the Lord, and his way does He will. Of the same Lord again it is said, It is God who works in you, even to will! Philippians 2:13 It is certain that it is we that act when we act; but it is He who makes us act, by applying efficacious powers to our will, who has said, I will make you to walk in my statutes, and to observe my judgments, and to do them. Ezekiel 36:27 When he says, I will make you . . . to do them, what else does He say in fact than, I will take away from you your heart of stone, from which used to arise your inability to act, and I will give you a heart of flesh, Ezekiel 36:26 in order that you may act? And what does this promise amount to but this: I will remove your hard heart, out of which you did not act, and I will give you an obedient heart, out of which you shall act? It is He who causes us to act, to whom the human suppliant says, Set a watch, O Lord, before my mouth. That is to say: Make or enable me, O Lord, to set a watch before my mouth—a benefit which he had already obtained from God who thus described its influence: I set a watch upon my mouth.

Chapter 33 — A Good Will May Be Small and Weak; An Ample Will, Great Love. Operating and Co-operating Grace.

He, therefore, who wishes to do God's commandment, but is unable, already possesses a good will, but as yet a small and weak one; he will, however, become able when he shall have acquired a great and robust will. When the martyrs did the great commandments which they obeyed, they acted by a great will,— that is, with great love. Of this love the Lord Himself thus speaks: Greater love has no man than this, that a man lay down his life for his friends. John 15:13 In accordance with this, the apostle also says, He that loves his neighbour has fulfilled the law. For this: You shall not commit adultery, You shall not kill, You shall not steal, You shall not covet; and if there be any other commandment, it is briefly comprehended in this saying, namely, You shall love your neighbour as yourself. Leviticus 19:18 Love works no ill to his neighbour: therefore love is the fulfilling of the law. Romans 13:8-10 This love the Apostle Peter did not yet possess, when he for fear thrice denied the Lord. Matthew 26:69-75 There is no fear in love, says the Evangelist John in his first Epistle, but perfect love casts out fear. 1 John 4:18 But yet, however small and imperfect his love was, it was not wholly wanting when he said to the Lord, I will lay down my life for Your sake; John 13:37 for he supposed himself able to effect what he felt himself willing to do. And who was it that had begun to give him his love, however small, but He who prepares the will, and perfects by His co-operation what He initiates by His operation? Forasmuch as in beginning He works in us that we may have the will, and in perfecting works with us when we have the will. On which account the apostle says, I am confident of this very thing, that He which has begun a good work in you will perform it until the day of Jesus Christ. Philippians 1:6 He operates, therefore, without us, in order that we may will; but when we will, and so will that we may act, He co-operates with us. We can, however, ourselves do nothing to effect good works of piety without Him either working that we may will, or co-working when we will. Now, concerning His working that we may will, it is said: It is God which works in you, even to will. Philippians 2:13 While of His co-working with us, when we will and act by willing, the apostle says, We know that in all things there is co-working for good to them that love God. What does this phrase, all things, mean, but the terrible and cruel sufferings which affect our condition? That burden, indeed, of Christ, which is heavy for our infirmity, becomes light to love. For to such did the Lord say that His burden was light, Matthew 11:30 as Peter was when he suffered for Christ, not as he was when he denied Him.

Chapter 34.— The Apostle's Eulogy of Love. Correction to Be Administered with Love.

This charity, that is, this will glowing with intensest love, the apostle eulogizes with these words: Who shall separate us from the love of Christ? Shall tribulation, or distress, or persecution, or famine, or nakedness, or peril, or the sword? (As it is written, For Your sake we are killed all the day long; we are accounted as sheep for the slaughter.) Nay, in all these things we are more than conquerors, through Him that loved us. For I am persuaded, that neither death, nor life, nor angels, nor principalities, nor things present, nor things to come, nor height, nor depth, nor any other creature, shall be able to separate us from the love of God, which is in Christ Jesus our Lord. Romans 8:35-39 And in another passage he says, And yet I show unto you a more excellent way. Though I speak with the tongues of men and of angels, and have not love, I have become as sounding brass, or a tinkling cymbal. And though I have the gift of prophecy, and understand all mysteries, and all knowledge; and though I have all faith, so that I could remove mountains, and have not love, I am nothing. And though I bestow all my goods to feed the poor, and though I give my body to be burned, and have not love, it profits me nothing. Love suffers long, and is kind; love envies not; love vaunts not itself, is not puffed up, does not behave itself unseemly, seeks not her own, is not easily provoked, thinks no evil; rejoices not in iniquity, but rejoices in the truth; bears all things, believes all things, hopes all things, endures all things. Love never fails. And a little afterwards he says, And now abides faith, hope, love, these three; but the greatest of these is love. Follow after love. He also says to the Galatians, For, brethren, you have been called unto liberty; only use not liberty for an occasion to the flesh, but by love serve one another. For all the law is fulfilled in one word, even in this, You shall love your neighbour as yourself. This is the same in effect as what he writes to the Romans: He that loves another has fulfilled the law. Romans 13:8 In like manner he says to the Colossians, And above all these things, put on love, which is the bond of perfectness. Colossians 3:14 And to Timothy he writes, Now the end of the commandment is love; and he goes on to describe the quality of this grace, saying, Out of a pure heart, and of a good conscience, and of faith unfeigned. 1 Timothy 1:5 Moreover, when he says to the Corinthians, Let all your things be done with love, 1 Corinthians 16:14 he shows plainly enough that even those chastisements which are deemed sharp and bitter by those who are corrected thereby, are to be administered with love. Accordingly, in another passage, after saying, Warn them that are unruly, comfort the feeble-minded, support the weak, be patient toward all men, he immediately added, See that none render evil for evil unto any man. 1 Thessalonians 5:14-15 Therefore, even when the unruly are corrected, it is not rendering evil for evil, but contrariwise, good. However, what but love works all these things?

Chapter 35.— Commendations of Love.

The Apostle Peter, likewise, says, And, above all things, have fervent love among yourselves: for love shall cover the multitude of sins. 1 Peter 4:8 The Apostle James also says, If you fulfil the royal law, according to the Scripture, You shall love your neighbour as yourself, you do well. James 2:8 So also the Apostle John says, He that loves his brother abides in the right; 1 John 2:10 again, in another passage, Whosoever does not righteousness is not of God, neither he that loves not his brother; for this is the message which we have heard from the beginning, that we should love one another. 1 John 3:10-11 Then he says again, This is His commandment, that we should believe in the name of His Son Jesus Christ, and love one another. 1 John 3:23 Once more: And this commandment have we from Him that he who loves God love his brother also. 1 John 4:21 Then shortly afterwards he adds, By this we know that we love the children of God, when we love God, and keep His commandments; for this is the love of God, that we keep His commandments: and His commandments are not grievous. 1 John 5:2-3 While, in his second Epistle, it is written, Not as though I wrote a new commandment unto you, but that which we had from the beginning, that we love one another.
Chapter 36.— Love Commended by Our Lord Himself.

Moreover, the Lord Jesus Himself teaches us that the whole law and the prophets hang upon the two precepts of love to God and love to our neighbour. Concerning these two commandments the following is written in the Gospel according to St. Mark: And one of the scribes came, and having heard them reasoning together, and perceiving that He had answered them well, asked Him: Which is the first commandment of all? And Jesus answered him: The first of all the commandments is, Hear, O Israel! The Lord our God is one Lord; and you shall love the Lord your God with all your heart, and with all your soul, and with all your mind, and with all your strength. Deuteronomy 6:4-5 This is the first commandment. And the second is like it: You shall love your neighbour as yourself. Leviticus 19:18 There is none other commandment greater than these. Mark 12:28-31 Also, in the Gospel according to St. John, He says, A new commandment I give unto you, that you love one another; as I have loved you, that you also love one another. By this shall all men know that you are my disciples, if you have love to one another. John 13:34-35

Chapter 37 — The Love Which Fulfils the Commandments is Not of Ourselves, But of God.

All these commandments, however, respecting love or charity (which are so great, and such that whatever action a man may think he does well is by no means well done if done without love) would be given to men in vain if they had not free choice of will. But forasmuch as these precepts are given in the law, both old and new (although in the new came the grace which was promised in the old, but the law without grace is the letter which kills, but in grace the Spirit which gives life), from what source is there in men the love of God and of one's neighbour but from God Himself? For indeed, if it be not of God but of men, the Pelagians have gained the victory; but if it come from God, then we have vanquished the Pelagians. Let, then, the Apostle John sit in judgment between us; and let him say to us, Beloved, let us love one another. 1 John 4:7 Now, when they begin to extol themselves on these words of John, and to ask why this precept is addressed to us at all if we have not of our own selves to love one another, the same apostle proceeds at once, to their confusion, to add, For love is of God. 1 John 4:7 It is not of ourselves, therefore, but it is of God. Wherefore, then, is it said, Let us love one another, for love is of God, unless it be as a precept to our free will, admonishing it to seek the gift of God? Now, this would be indeed a thoroughly fruitless admonition if the will did not previously receive some donation of love, which might seek to be enlarged so as to fulfil whatever command was laid upon it. When it is said, Let us love one another, it is law; when it is said, For love is of God, it is grace. For God's wisdom carries law and mercy upon her tongue. Proverbs 3:16 Accordingly, it is written in the Psalm, For He who gave the law will give blessings.

Chapter 38.— We Would Not Love God Unless He First Loved Us. The Apostles Chose Christ Because They Were Chosen; They Were Not Chosen Because They Chose Christ.

Let no one, then, deceive you, my brethren, for we should not love God unless He first loved us. John again gives us the plainest proof of this when he says, We love Him because He first loved us. 1 John 4:19 Grace makes us lovers of the law; but the law itself, without grace, makes us nothing but breakers of the law. And nothing else than this is shown us by the words of our Lord when He says to His disciples, You have not chosen me, but I have chosen you. John 15:16 For if we first loved Him, in order that by this merit He might love us, then we first chose Him that we might deserve to be chosen by Him. He, however, who is the Truth says otherwise, and flatly contradicts this vain conceit of men. You have not chosen me, He says. If, therefore, you have not chosen me, undoubtedly you have not loved me (for how could they choose one whom they did not love?). But I, says He, have chosen you. And then could they possibly help choosing Him afterwards, and preferring Him to all the blessings of this world? But it was because they had been chosen, that they chose Him; not because they chose Him that they were chosen. There could be no merit in men's choice of Christ, if it were not that God's grace was prevenient in His choosing them. Whence the Apostle Paul pronounces in the Thessalonians this benediction: The Lord make you to increase and abound in love one toward another, and toward all men. 1 Thessalonians 3:12 This benediction to love one another He gave us, who had also given us a law that we should love each other. Then, in another passage addressed to the same church, seeing that there now existed in some of its members the disposition which he had wished them to cultivate, he says, We are bound to thank God always for you, brethren, as it is meet, because that your faith grows exceedingly, and the charity of every one of you all toward each other abounds. 2 Thessalonians 1:3 This he said lest they should make a boast of the great good which they were enjoying from God, as if they had it of their own mere selves. Because, then, your faith has so great a growth (this is the purport of his words), and the love of every one of you all toward each other so greatly abounds, we ought to thank God concerning you, but not to praise you, as if you possessed these gifts of yourselves.

Chapter 39.— The Spirit of Fear a Great Gift of God.

The apostle also says to Timothy, For God has not given to us the spirit of fear, but of power, and of love, and of a sound mind. 2 Timothy 1:7 Now in respect of this passage of the apostle, we must be on our guard against supposing that we have not received the spirit of the fear of God, which is undoubtedly a great gift of God, and concerning which the prophet Isaiah says, The Spirit of the Lord shall rest upon you, the spirit of wisdom and understanding, the spirit of counsel and might, the spirit of knowledge and piety, the spirit of the fear of the Lord. Isaiah 11:2 It is not the fear with which Peter denied Christ that we have received the spirit of, but that fear concerning which Christ Himself says, Fear Him who has power to destroy both soul and body in hell; yea, I say unto you, Fear Him. Luke 12:5 This, indeed, He said, lest we should deny Him from the same fear which shook Peter; for such cowardice he plainly wished to be removed from us when He, in the preceding passage, said, Be not afraid of them that kill the body, and after that have no more that they can do. Luke 12:4 It is not of this fear that we have received the spirit, but of power, and of love, and of a sound mind. And of this spirit the same Apostle Paul discourses to the Romans: We glory in tribulations, knowing that tribulation works patience; and patience, experience; and experience, hope; and hope makes not ashamed; because the love of God is shed abroad in our hearts by the Holy Ghost, which is given unto us. Not by ourselves, therefore, but by the Holy Ghost which is given to us, does it come to pass that, through that very love, which he shows us to be the gift of God, tribulation does not do away with patience, but rather produces it. Again, he says to the Ephesians, Peace be to the brethren, and love with faith. Ephesians 6:23 Great blessings these! Let him tell us, however, whence they come. From God the Father, says he immediately afterwards, and the Lord Jesus Christ. John 1:5 These great blessings, therefore, are nothing else than God's gifts to us.

Chapter 40 — The Ignorance of the Pelagians in Maintaining that the Knowledge of the Law Comes from God, But that Love Comes from Ourselves.

It is no wonder that light shines in darkness, and the darkness comprehends it not. John 1:5 In John's Epistle the Light declares, Behold what manner of love the Father has bestowed upon us, that we should be called the sons of God. 1 John 3:1 And in the Pelagian writings the darkness says, Love comes to us of our own selves. Now, if they only possessed the true, that is, Christian love, they would also know whence they obtained possession of it; even as the apostle knew when he said, But we have received not the spirit of the world, but the Spirit which is of God, that we might know the things that are freely given to us of God. 1 Corinthians 2:12 John says, God is love. 1 John 4:16 And thus the Pelagians affirm that they actually have God Himself, not from God, but from their own selves! And although they allow that we have the knowledge of the law from God, they will yet have it that love is from our very selves. Nor do they listen to the apostle when he says, Knowledge puffs up, but love edifies. 1 Corinthians 8:1 Now what can be more absurd, nay, what more insane and more alien from the very sacredness of love itself, than to maintain that from God proceeds the knowledge which, apart from love, puffs us up, while the love which prevents the possibility of this inflation of knowledge springs from ourselves? And again, when the apostle speaks of the love of Christ as surpassing knowledge, Ephesians 3:19 what can be more insane than to suppose that the knowledge which must be subordinated to love comes from God, while the love which surpasses knowledge comes from man? The true faith, however, and sound doctrine declare that both graces are from God; the Scripture says, From His face comes knowledge and understanding; Proverbs 2:6 and another Scripture says, Love is of God. 1 John 4:7 We read of the Spirit of wisdom and understanding. Isaiah 11:2 Also of the Spirit of power, and of love, and of a sound mind. 2 Timothy 1:7 But love is a greater gift than knowledge; for whenever a man has the gift of knowledge, love is necessary by the side of it, that he be not puffed up. For love envies not, vaunts not itself, is not puffed up. 1 Corinthians 13:4

Chapter 41— The Wills of Men are So Much in the Power of God, that He Can Turn Them Whithersoever It Pleases Him.

I think I have now discussed the point fully enough in opposition to those who vehemently oppose the grace of God, by which, however, the human will is not taken away, but changed from bad to good, and assisted when it is good. I think, too, that I have so discussed the subject, that it is not so much I myself as the inspired Scripture which has spoken to you, in the clearest testimonies of truth; and if this divine record be looked into carefully, it shows us that not only men's good wills, which God Himself converts from bad ones, and, when converted by Him, directs to good actions and to eternal life, but also those which follow the world are so entirely at the disposal of God, that He turns them wherever He wills, and whenever He wills,— to bestow kindness on some, and to heap punishment on others, as He Himself judges right by a counsel most secret to Himself, indeed, but beyond all doubt most righteous. For we find that some sins are even the punishment of other sins, as are those vessels of wrath which the apostle describes as fitted to destruction; Romans 9:22 as is also that hardening of Pharaoh, the purpose of which is said to be to set forth in him the power of God; as, again, is the flight of the Israelites from the face of the enemy before the city of Ai, for fear arose in their heart so that they fled, and this was done that their sin might be punished in the way it was right that it should be; by reason of which the Lord said to Joshua the son of Nun, The children of Israel shall not be able to stand before the face of their enemies. What is the meaning of, They shall not be able to stand? Now, why did they not stand by free will, but, with a will perplexed by fear, took to flight, were it not that God has the lordship even over men's wills, and when He is angry turns to fear whomsoever He pleases? Was it not of their own will that the enemies of the children of Israel fought against the people of God, as led by Joshua, the son of Nun? And yet the Scripture says, It was of the Lord to harden their hearts, that they should come against Israel in battle, that they might be exterminated. Joshua 11:20 And was it not likewise of his own will that the wicked son of Gera cursed King David? And yet what says David, full of true, and deep, and pious wisdom? What did he say to him who wanted to smite the reviler? What, said he, have I to do with you, you sons of Zeruiah? Let him alone and let him curse, because the Lord has said unto him, Curse David. Who, then, shall say, Wherefore have you done so? 2 Samuel 16:9-10 And then the inspired Scripture, as if it would confirm the king's profound utterance by repeating it once more, tells us: And David said to Abishai, and to all his servants, Behold, my son, which came forth from my bowels, seeks my life: how much more may this Benjamite do it! Let him alone, and let him curse; for the Lord has bidden him. It may be that the Lord will look on my humiliation, and will requite me good for his cursing this day. 2 Samuel 16:11-12 Now what prudent reader will fail to understand in what way the Lord bade this profane man to curse David? It was not by a command that He bade him, in which case his obedience would be praiseworthy; but He inclined the man's will, which had become debased by his own perverseness, to commit this sin, by His own just and secret judgment. Therefore it is said, The Lord said unto him. Now if this person had obeyed a command of God, he would have deserved to be praised rather than punished, as we know he was afterwards punished for this sin. Nor is the reason an obscure one why the Lord told him after this manner to curse David. It may be, said the humbled king, that the Lord will look on my humiliation, and will requite me good for his cursing this day. See, then, what proof we have here that God uses the hearts of even wicked men for the praise and assistance of the good. Thus did He make use of Judas when betraying Christ; thus did He make use of the Jews when they crucified Christ. And how vast the blessings which from these instances He has bestowed upon the nations that should believe in Him! He also uses our worst enemy, the devil himself, but in the best way, to exercise and try the faith and piety of good men,— not for Himself indeed, who knows all things before they come to pass, but for our sakes, for whom it was necessary that such a discipline should be gone through with us. Did not Absalom choose by his own will the counsel which was detrimental to him? And yet the reason of his doing so was that the Lord had heard his father's prayer that it might be so. Wherefore the Scripture says that the Lord appointed to defeat the good counsel of Ahithophel, to the intent that the Lord might bring all evils upon Absalom. 2 Samuel 17:14 It called Ahithophel's counsel good, because it was for the moment of advantage to his purpose. It was in favour of the son against his father, against whom he had rebelled; and it might have crushed him, had not the Lord defeated the counsel which Ahithophel had given, by acting on the heart of Absalom so that he rejected this counsel, and chose another which was not expedient for him.

Chapter 42 — God Does Whatsoever He Wills in the Hearts of Even Wicked Men.

Who can help trembling at those judgments of God by which He does in the hearts of even wicked men whatsoever He wills, at the same time rendering to them according to their deeds? Rehoboam, the son of Solomon, rejected the salutary counsel of the old men, not to deal harshly with the people, and preferred listening to the words of the young men of his own age, by returning a rough answer to those to whom he should have spoken gently. Now whence arose such conduct, except from his own will? Upon this, however, the ten tribes of Israel revolted from him, and chose for themselves another king, even Jeroboam, that the will of God in His anger might be accomplished which He had predicted would come to pass. 1 Kings 12:8-14 For what says the Scripture? The king hearkened not unto the people; for the turning was from the Lord, that He might perform His saying, which the Lord spoke to Ahijah the Shilonite concerning Jeroboam the son of Nebat. 1 Kings 12:15 All this, indeed, was done by the will of man, although the turning was from the Lord. Read the books of the Chronicles, and you will find the following passage in the second book: Moreover, the Lord stirred up against Jehoram the spirit of the Philistines, and of the Arabians, that were neighbours to the Ethiopians; and they came up to the land of Judah, and ravaged it, and carried away all the substance which was found in the king's house. 2 Chronicles 21:16-17 Here it is shown that God stirs up enemies to devastate the countries which He adjudges deserving of such chastisement. Still, did these Philistines and Arabians invade the land of Judah to waste it with no will of their own? Or were their movements so directed by their own will that the Scripture lies which tells us that the Lord stirred up their spirit to do all this? Both statements to be sure are true, because they both came by their own will, and yet the Lord stirred up their spirit; and this may also with equal truth be stated the other way: The Lord both stirred up their spirit, and yet they came of their own will. For the Almighty sets in motion even in the innermost hearts of men the movement of their will, so that He does through their agency whatsoever He wishes to perform through them—even

He who knows not how to will anything in unrighteousness. What, again, is the purport of that which the man of God said to King Amaziah: Let not the army of Israel go with you; for the Lord is not with Israel, even with all the children of Ephraim: for if you shall think to obtain with these, the Lord shall put you to flight before your enemies: for God has power either to strengthen or to put to flight? 2 Chronicles 25:7-8 Now, how does the power of God help some in war by giving them confidence, and put others to flight by injecting fear into them, except it be that He who has made all things according to His own will, in heaven and on earth, also works in the hearts of men? We read also what Joash, king of Israel, said when he sent a message to Amaziah, king of Judah, who wanted to fight with him. After certain other words, he added, Now tarry at home; why do you challenge me to your hurt, that you should fall, even you, and Judah with you? 2 Kings 14:10 Then the Scripture has added this sequel: But Amaziah would not hear; for it came of God, that he might be delivered into their hands, because they sought after the gods of Edom. 2 Chronicles 25:20 Behold, now, how God, wishing to punish the sin of idolatry, wrought this in this man's heart, with whom He was indeed justly angry, not to listen to sound advice, but to despise it, and go to the battle, in which he with his army was routed. God says by the prophet Ezekiel, If the prophet be deceived when he has spoken a thing, I the Lord have deceived that prophet: I will stretch out my hand upon him, and will destroy him from the midst of my people Israel. Ezekiel 14:9 Then there is the book of Esther, who was a woman of the people of Israel, and in the land of their captivity became the wife of the foreign King Ahasuerus. In this book it is written, that, being driven by necessity to interpose in behalf of her people, whom the king had ordered to be slain in every part of his dominions, she prayed to the Lord. So strongly was she urged by the necessity of the case, that she even ventured into the royal presence without the king's command, and contrary to her own custom. Now observe what the Scripture says: He looked at her like a bull in the vehemence of his indignation; and the queen was afraid, and her colour changed as she fainted; and she bowed herself upon the head of her delicate maiden which went before her. But God turned the king, and transformed his indignation into gentleness. The Scripture says in the Proverbs of Solomon, Even as the rush of water, so is the heart of a king in God's hand; He will turn it in whatever way He shall choose. Proverbs 21:1 Again, in the 104th Psalm, in reference to the Egyptians, one reads what God did to them:

And He turned their heart to hate His people, to deal subtly with His servants. Observe, likewise, what is written in the letters of the apostles. In the Epistle of Paul, the Apostle, to the Romans occur these words: Wherefore God gave them up to uncleanness, through the lusts of their own hearts; Romans 1:24 and a little afterwards: For this cause God gave them up unto vile affections; Romans 1:26 again, in the next passage: And even as they did not like to retain God in their knowledge, God gave them over to a reprobate mind, to do those things which are not convenient. Romans 1:28 So also in his second Epistle to the Thessalonians, the apostle says of sundry persons, Inasmuch as they received not the love of the truth, that they might be saved; therefore also God shall send them strong delusion, that they should believe a lie; that they all might be judged who believed not the truth, but had pleasure in unrighteousness. 2 Thessalonians 2:10-12

Chapter 43.— God Operates on Men's Hearts to Incline Their Wills Whithersoever He Pleases.

From these statements of the inspired word, and from similar passages which it would take too long to quote in full, it is, I think, sufficiently clear that God works in the hearts of men to incline their wills wherever He wills, whether to good deeds according to His mercy, or to evil after their own deserts; His own judgment being sometimes manifest, sometimes secret, but always righteous. This ought to be the fixed and immoveable conviction of your heart, that there is no unrighteousness with God. Therefore, whenever you read in the Scriptures of Truth, that men are led aside, or that their hearts are blunted and hardened by God, never doubt that some ill deserts of their own have first occurred, so that they justly suffer these things. Thus you will not run counter to that proverb of Solomon: The foolishness of a man perverts his ways, yet he blames God in his heart. Proverbs 19:3 Grace, however, is not bestowed according to men's deserts; otherwise grace would be no longer grace. Romans 11:6 For grace is so designated because it is given gratuitously. Now if God is able, either through the agency of angels (whether good ones or evil), or in any other way whatever, to operate in the hearts even of the wicked, in return for their deserts,— whose wickedness was not made by Him, but was either derived originally from Adam, or increased by their own will,— what is there to wonder at if, through the Holy Spirit,

He works good in the hearts of the elect, who has wrought it that their hearts become good instead of evil?

Chapter 44 — Gratuitous Grace Exemplified in Infants.

Men, however, may suppose that there are certain good deserts which they think are precedent to justification through God's grace; all the while failing to see, when they express such an opinion, that they do nothing else than deny grace. But, as I have already remarked, let them suppose what they like respecting the case of adults, in the case of infants, at any rate, the Pelagians find no means of answering the difficulty. For these in receiving grace have no will; from the influence of which they can pretend to any precedent merit. We see, moreover, how they cry and struggle when they are baptized, and feel the divine sacraments. Such conduct would, of course, be charged against them as a great impiety, if they already had free will in use; and notwithstanding this, grace cleaves to them even in their resisting struggles. But most certainly there is no prevenient merit, otherwise the grace would be no longer grace. Sometimes, too, this grace is bestowed upon the children of unbelievers, when they happen by some means or other to fall, by reason of God's secret providence, into the hands of pious persons; but, on the other hand, the children of believers fail to obtain grace, some hindrance occurring to prevent the approach of help to rescue them in their danger. These things, no doubt, happen through the secret providence of God, whose judgments are unsearchable, and His ways past finding out. These are the words of the apostle; and you should observe what he had previously said, to lead him to add such a remark. He was discoursing about the Jews and Gentiles, when he wrote to the Romans— themselves Gentiles— to this effect: For as you, in times past, have not believed God, yet have now obtained mercy through their unbelief; even so have these also now not believed, that through your mercy they also may obtain mercy; for God has concluded them all in unbelief, that He might have mercy upon all. Romans 11:30-32 Now, after he had thought upon what he said, full of wonder at the certain truth of his own assertion, indeed, but astonished at its great depth, how God concluded all in unbelief that He might have mercy upon all—as if doing evil that good might come—he at once exclaimed, and said, O the depth of the riches both of the wisdom and knowledge of God! How unsearchable are His judgments, and His ways past finding out! Romans 11:33 Perverse men, who do not reflect upon these unsearchable judgments and untraceable ways, indeed, but are ever prone to censure, being unable to understand, have supposed the apostle to say, and censoriously gloried over him for saying, Let us do evil, that good may come! God forbid that the apostle should say so! But men, without understanding, have thought that this was in fact said, when they heard these words of the apostle: Moreover, the law entered, that the offense might abound; but where sin abounded, grace did much more abound. Romans 5:20 But grace, indeed, effects this purpose— that good works should now be wrought by those who previously did evil; not that they should persevere in evil courses and suppose that they are recompensed with good. Their language, therefore, ought not to be: Let us do evil, that good may come; but: We have done evil, and good has come; let us henceforth do good, that in the future world we may receive good for good, who in the present life are receiving good for evil. Wherefore it is written in the Psalm, I will sing of mercy and judgment unto You, O Lord. When the Son of man, therefore, first came into the world, it was not to judge the world, but that the world through Him might be saved. John 3:17 And this dispensation was for mercy; by and by, however, He will come for judgment— to judge the quick and the dead. And yet even in this present time salvation itself does not eventuate without judgment— although it be a hidden one; therefore He says, For judgment I have come into this world, that they which see not may see, and that they which see may be made blind. John 9:39

Chapter 45 — The Reason Why One Person is Assisted by Grace, and Another is Not Helped, Must Be Referred to the Secret Judgments of God.

You must refer the matter, then, to the hidden determinations of God, when you see, in one and the same condition, such as all infants unquestionably have—who derive their hereditary evil from Adam,— that one is assisted so as to be baptized, and another is not assisted, so that he dies in his very bondage; and again, that one baptized person is left and forsaken in his present life, who God foreknew would be ungodly, while another baptized person is taken away from this life, lest that wickedness should alter his understanding; Wisdom 4:11 and be sure that you do not in such cases ascribe unrighteousness or unwisdom to God, in whom is the very fountain of righteousness and wisdom, but, as I have exhorted you from the commencement of this treatise, whereto you have already attained, walk therein, and even this shall God reveal unto you, Philippians 3:15 — if not in this life, yet certainly in the next, for there is nothing covered that shall not be revealed. Matthew 10:26 When, therefore, you hear the Lord say, I the Lord have deceived that prophet, Ezekiel 14:9 and likewise what the apostle says: He has mercy on whom He will have mercy, and whom He will He hardens, Romans 9:18 believe that, in the case of him whom He permits to be deceived and hardened, his evil deeds have deserved the judgment; while in the case of him to whom He shows mercy, you should loyally and unhesitatingly recognise the grace of the God who renders not evil for evil; but contrariwise blessing. 1 Peter 3:9 Nor should you take away from Pharaoh free will, because in several passages God says, I have hardened Pharaoh; or, I have hardened or I will harden Pharaoh's heart; for it does not by any means follow that Pharaoh did not, on this account, harden his own heart. For this, too, is said of him, after the removal of the fly-plague from the Egyptians, in these words of the Scripture: And Pharaoh hardened his heart at this time also; neither would he let the people go. Exodus 8:32 Thus it was that both God hardened him by His just judgment, and Pharaoh by his own free will. Be then well assured that your labour will never be in vain, if, setting before you a good purpose, you persevere in it to the last. For God, who fails to render, according to their deeds, only to those whom He liberates, will then recompense every man according to his works. Matthew 16:27 God will, therefore, certainly recompense both evil for evil, because He is just; and good for evil, because He is good; and good for good, because He is good and just; only, evil for good He will never recompense, because He is not unjust. He will, therefore, recompense evil for evil— punishment for unrighteousness; and He will recompense good for evil— grace for unrighteousness; and He will recompense good for good— grace for grace.

Chapter 46 — Understanding and Wisdom Must Be Sought from God.

Peruse attentively this treatise, and if you understand it, give God the praise; but where you fail to understand it, pray for understanding, for God will give you understanding. Remember what the Scriptures say: If any of you lack wisdom, let him ask of God, who gives to all men liberally, and upbraids not; and it shall be given to him. James 1:5 Wisdom itself comes down from above, as the Apostle James himself tells us. There is, however, another wisdom, which you must repel from you, and pray against its remaining in you; this the same apostle expressed his detestation of when he said, But if you have bitter envying and strife in your hearts, . . . this is not the wisdom which descends from above, but is earthly, sensual, devilish. For wherever there is envying and strife, there is also confusion, and every evil work. But the wisdom which is from above is first pure, then peaceable, gentle, and easy to be entreated, full of mercy and good works, without partiality, and without hypocrisy. James 3:14-17 What blessing, then, will that man not have who has prayed for this wisdom and obtained it of the Lord? And from this you may understand what grace is; because if this wisdom were of ourselves, it would not be from above; nor would it be an object to be asked for of the God who created us. Brethren, pray ye for us also, that we may live soberly, righteously, and godly in this present world; looking for that blessed hope, and the glorious appearing of our Lord and Saviour Jesus Christ, Titus 2:12 to whom belong the honour, and the glory, and the kingdom, with the Father and the Holy Ghost, for ever and ever. Amen.

Printed in Great Britain
by Amazon.co.uk, Ltd.,
Marston Gate.